D0457290

SOCIAL MEDIA FOR SOCIAL GOOD

*A How-To Guide
for Nonprofits*

HEATHER MANSFIELD

New York   Chicago   San Francisco
Lisbon   London   Madrid   Mexico City   Milan
New Delhi   San Juan   Seoul   Singapore
Sydney   Toronto

The **McGraw·Hill** Companies

Copyright © 2012 by The McGraw-Hill Companies. All rights reserved. Printed in
the United States of America. Except as permitted under the United States Copyright Act of 1976, no part of this publication may be reproduced or distributed in
any form or by any means, or stored in a database or retrieval system, without the
prior written permission of the publisher.

1 2 3 4 5 6 7 8 9 0   QFR/QFR   1 6 5 4 3 2 1

ISBN   978-0-07-177081-1
MHID   0-07-177081-X

e-ISBN   978-0-07-177099-6
e-MHID   0-07-177099-2

Product or brand names used in this book may be trade names or trademarks.
Where we believe that there may be proprietary claims to such trade names or
trademarks, the name has been used with an initial capital or it has been capital-
ized in the style used by the name claimant. Regardless of the capitalization used,
all such names have been used in an editorial manner without any intent to convey endorsement of or other affiliation with the name claimant. Neither the au-
thor nor the publisher intends to express any judgment as to the validity or legal
status of any such proprietary claims.

McGraw-Hill books are available at special quantity discounts to use as premiums
and sales promotions, or for use in corporate training programs. To contact a
representative please e-mail us at bulksales@mcgraw-hill.com.

This book is printed on acid-free paper.

This book is dedicated to all the nonprofit staff and volunteers worldwide who Tweet, Share, Update, Friend, Like, Check-in, Join, Connect, and Post for Social Good. The world is a better place because of you.

CONTENTS

PART 2   WEB 2.0: THE SOCIAL WEB

CHAPTER
5

YOUTUBE AND FLICKR 115

CHAPTER
6

LINKEDIN 137

CHAPTER 7

BLOGGING 155

PART 3 WEB 3.0: THE MOBILE WEB

CHAPTER 8

SOCIAL MEDIA AND THE MOBILE WEB 177

CHAPTER 9

MOBILE WEBSITES 201

CHAPTER 10

GROUP TEXT MESSAGING AND
TEXT-TO-GIVE TECHNOLOGY 217

INTRODUCTION

INTEGRATING WEB 1.0, WEB 2.0, AND WEB 3.0

The Internet has come a long way in the last 15 years. Back in 1997, while I was volunteering with a school for street children in Guatemala, I launched my first online fundraising campaign, using only a Yahoo! e-mail account. I had no digital camera or smartphone, no blog or Facebook profile, no PayPal account. None of those tools existed yet. From Internet cafés, I began telling my family and friends the stories of the children and their need for clothing and medicine and asked them to write and snail mail checks to a close friend in California, who then wired the funds to a bank in Guatemala. All told, a little over $400 was raised, which went a long way in Guatemala at the time (and still does) and did a great deal of good for the children—good that would not have happened had it not been for the Internet.

That experience led me to fall in love with the Web and its potential for social good. I was young(er), passionate, and motivated (and saddened) because so many people were suffering unjustly. I believed deeply that the Internet could change our world for the better and help alleviate that suffering if we could discover ways of using it that would inspire and thus mobilize the masses to take action and to give. I still believe that. I have watched the rise of websites, e-newsletters, donate now technology, and e-mail advocacy in the years that followed that first online fundraising campaign, and those tools have empowered nonprofits like no others before them. It was a very exciting time to be in nonprofit communications and fundraising.

Then came social media. I joined Myspace in 2005, and within three minutes of browsing, I had the exact same epiphanic moment of clarity that I had had with Yahoo! and e-mail fundraising—this is going to change everything. And it has. Nonprofits and their status updates and tweets have filtered into almost every content area of the Web. Nonprofits have become omnipresent online. They are leading communities of millions worldwide who are unified in the common goal of making life better for people, animals, and the Earth. In the whole scheme of things, 15 years of Internet history is a drop in the bucket, but today, in the era of the Social Web, we are truly beginning to witness and experience the power and potential of the Internet for social good.

Now, in 2011, we are on the brink of yet another great shift in communications and fundraising technology. The Web is going mobile. Without a magic crystal ball, it is almost impossible to know where nonprofit communications will be by 2015, but it's thrilling to ponder. There are tools that do not yet exist that will propel nonprofits and connect advocates for social good in ways that our brains can't even imagine yet, and similar to my e-mail fundraising and Myspace moments of clarity, the purchase of my first iPhone in 2009 made me realize yet again, this is going to change everything.

During my professional career, I have experienced the birth of three separate eras of nonprofit Web communications and fundraising. Each era has come with its own unique set of tools and best practices. However, they are complementary in nature. One era does not replace the previous one. In fact, when a nonprofit successfully integrates the tools and best practices from all three eras into one comprehensive, integrated communications and fundraising strategy, the potential for social good is multiplied exponentially. And that, friends, followers, and fans, is the purpose of this book: to help you make sense of these three eras, their distinct tool sets, how they affect one another, and how they can be integrated successfully and cost-effectively to maximize your nonprofit's return on investment (ROI) and its contribution to the greater social good. For the sake of clarity, the three eras of non-profit Web communications and fundraising are defined in this book as follows:

- *Web 1.0: the Static Web.* This is best characterized as broadcasting from one to many. Web 1.0 tools for nonprofits include their websites, e-newsletters, "Donate Now" buttons, and e-advocacy campaigns. These tools still result in the highest ROI in terms of dollars raised. Your nonprofit should give the highest priority to the effective implementation and management of these tools before branching out into using Web 2.0 and Web 3.0 tools.

- *Web 2.0: the Social Web.* This is best described as an evolution from broadcasting to supporters to engaging with them. Web 2.0 tools for the nonprofit sector are primarily social networking sites, blogging platforms, and peer-to-peer fundraising tools. The ROI from Web 2.0 tools can be very high if they are successfully integrated into your Web 1.0 campaigns. You build community by interacting with your supporters online, but you also want to encourage them to visit your website, sign up for your e-newsletter, make an online donation, and participate in e-advocacy campaigns.

- *Web 3.0: the Mobile Web.* This era combines the tools of the previous two, but enables them to be experienced on mobile devices anywhere at any time. Additionally, group text messaging, text-to-give technology, mobile websites, and smartphone and tablet apps are uniquely Web 3.0, but I believe that many of the tools that will come to characterize this era do not exist yet. They are being conceptualized and built by social entrepreneurs worldwide at this very moment. Strategically, before rushing into Web 3.0, your nonprofit should have the building blocks of Web 1.0 and Web 2.0 tools in place. Your potential success with pioneering the Mobile Web depends upon this.

THIS BOOK IS YOUR STRATEGIC PLAN

The knowledge presented in this book is based upon 15 years of online communications and fundraising experience and upon research gleaned from interviews with nonprofits and discussions on LinkedIn, Facebook, Twitter, and my blog, *Nonprofit Tech 2.0* (nonprofitorgsblog.org). It is written chapter by chapter as a to-do list of sorts, and it is meant to serve as a foundation for your Web 1.0, Web 2.0, and Web 3.0 strategic plans. The best practices were learned and earned through trial and error, and have directly resulted in the "Nonprofit Organizations" communities on Facebook, Twitter, YouTube, Flickr, LinkedIn, Myspace, and Foursquare growing to more than half a million friends, followers, and fans. Actually, the fact that you are reading this book now, that it exists, is testament to the power of the best practices outlined in this book and the tools available to nonprofits today.

It is my hope that you will read each chapter carefully and implement the best practices that make sense for your nonprofit. Most of the best practices discussed are applicable to all nonprofits, but in some cases, you will find that you need to use your best judgment concerning their applicability to your nonprofit's mission, programs, and supporters in order to gauge their potential effectiveness. At the back of this book, there is a "Nonprofit Tech Checklist" that will help you stay organized. Please make a copy and keep it somewhere close so that you can check off the various items and monitor your progress. To utilize every tool and best practice on this checklist could take 12 to 24 months. Don't let yourself be overwhelmed by this. As long as you have the will, you have the time. Also, at the end of each chapter is a "Google This!" section. When searched for, the keywords and phrases listed there will provide you with direct access to important resources and information. Please take the time to complete the research and check off the keywords and phrases as you go along. Finally, also at the end of each chapter, you'll find a list of nonprofits that excel on the topic(s) covered in that chapter. They have been selected because they have implemented the best practices covered in this book. Please visit the links provided so that you can see real-time examples of nonprofit excellence in Web 1.0, Web 2.0, and Web 3.0 communications and fundraising.

Many nonprofits are confounded by the dramatic changes in online communications and fundraising in recent years, and are overwhelmed by the explosion of new social media and mobile technology tools that are now available. Which should we prioritize? How much time will they take? How much do the tools cost? Will they result in online donations? Do we need to hire someone? Do we still need to be publishing print materials? You'll find the answers to all those questions in this book. It cuts through the hype and clearly defines what the value of social media and mobile technology is and where the ROI from today's online communications and fundraising trends can be found. That said, before you begin, you must understand several things from the outset.

Technology Is Now Constantly in Flux

You will need to be adaptable. The Web and the tools themselves are constantly changing. Technology moves much faster now and shows no signs of slowing down. You have to accept that your work will never be done. There will always be upgrades to be made and new tools to experiment with. That said, the person who is best suited to manage your online communications and fundraising campaigns will embrace and relish this new reality, rather than bemoan it.

There Is No Customer Service

Unless you are paying a monthly or an annual fee, you should not expect customer service. Social networking communities like Facebook, Twitter, and Foursquare probably receive tens of thousands of questions a day via e-mail. That means that in most cases, you are on your own in finding answers to your questions through Google searches, FAQs, Help forums, or the blogosphere.

These Tools Are Low-Cost, but Not Free

There are countless tools available to the nonprofit sector today that are either free or low-cost, and their value should not be underestimated. Tools like WordPress, Facebook, Twitter, YouTube, and Foursquare have helped level the playing field in the nonprofit sector. With proper training, any nonprofit of any size can launch and maintain exceptional Web 1.0, Web 2.0, and Web 3.0 campaigns on a small budget. That said, such campaigns are not possible without investing resources in additional staff members. Development and communications staff members whose job descriptions are already lengthy cannot be expected to also serve as your nonprofit's social media and mobile technology manager(s). Interns and volunteers are wonderful assistants, but if they are untrained, most often they do not have the necessary experience to use these tools effectively.

Fear Is Counterproductive in Social Media

Enough with the fear! Learn how to navigate and utilize new Web technologies, or risk becoming irrelevant. If your nonprofit serves minors or any constituency for which privacy is paramount, then approach social media with caution and practicality. Otherwise, the hard truth is that social media is no longer new. Many early adopters are already moving on to the Mobile Web. If your nonprofit is still in the should-we-or-shouldn't-we stage, you are quickly falling behind. It is a Brave New Web, and it's time to muster the courage and take the leap.

Community Building Is Never a Waste of Time

Social networking communities are migrant communities. If you build a community on a social networking site and that site then falls in popularity, the time you invested in building that community was not wasted because that community will most likely move with you to the Next Big Thing. For example, when Myspace started to lose popularity, I began moving that community over to Facebook and Twitter, and now I have vibrant, thriving communities on both sites. The trick is to know when a community is beginning to lose its gusto and then mobilize that community to move on quickly. That's why it is so important that you diversify your online brand by building multiple communities. If one community goes down, you have a backup. The online commons is fickle. Never assume that a community, even Facebook, is forever.

Five Thousand Is the Magic Number

Communities begin to grow exponentially when they reach 5,000 members. I've observed this phenomenon on Facebook, Twitter, LinkedIn, Myspace, and Foursquare. From there on out, the larger your community gets, the faster it grows. Large national and international nonprofits have little problem reaching this benchmark, but small and some medium-size nonprofits will. Some will say that the number of likes or followers that you have doesn't matter, but it does. The larger your communities, the higher your ROI. Work toward that goal of 5,000. It may take a year or two, but if you follow the best practices in this book, you will reach that magic number.

NONPROFITS WERE THE EARLY ADOPTERS

As mentioned earlier, I started my work in social media in February of 2005 by joining Myspace and creating the "Nonprofit Organizations" Myspace Profile, and in the years since, I have conducted trainings and run social media campaigns for small businesses, institutions of higher education, and nonprofit organizations. Having spent a minimum of 50 hours a week on social media sites since 2005, I have watched all three sectors grow and evolve in their use of social media, and I am compelled to give credit where credit is due. The blogosphere and the media like to sing the praises of the business sector and its use of social media, but they do not acknowledge often enough that it was nonprofits that ushered in the era of the Social Web. While big corporate brands and institutions of higher education were having meetings (and panic attacks) about whether they should risk using social media, nonprofits were already active on Myspace, YouTube, Flickr, and Facebook.

It's one thing for a large corporate brand to be successful on social media (because it is a large corporate brand!), but it's quite another for a nonprofit with no budget and a little-known brand name to be successful. For the most part, nonprofits' use of social media has been underestimated by the business sector, when in fact businesses could learn quite a lot from us. I always like to point out that nonprofits are the best sales reps on the planet. When a business sells a product online for $20, the buyer gets something tangible in return, like this book, a T-shirt, or a piece of jewelry. A $20 online donation only results in the buyer's having a sense that she is making the world a better place. That's a much harder sell, especially while struggling through a global economic recession, and yet online giving is rising faster than ever, in direct correlation with the rise of social media in the nonprofit sector. Nonprofits should be proud of their achievements in social media and their pioneering of the Social Web for social good.

Institutions of higher education, however, had a very slow start in social media in comparison to the nonprofit and business sectors, and they paid a price for this. Colleges and universities were terrified of losing control of their online messaging, and while they weren't participating, current students and alumni were creating communities for their colleges and universities on Myspace, Facebook, and YouTube. You can't imagine (or maybe you can) the freak-outs that followed when administrative and marketing staff members at colleges and universities discovered that they had large, active communities on social networking sites that were completely out of their control. Thankfully, by the time Twitter had become popular in 2008, institutions of higher education had woken up and begun to embrace the Social Web, but not without some serious growing pains along the way. This fear factor is often brought up when discussing the nonprofit sector and social media, but the nonprofits' fear level was minimal compared to that found in higher education. That said, credit must also be given to the librarians in institutions of higher education. In 2006 and 2007, they bravely launched communities on Myspace, Facebook, and YouTube without permission because they knew that they probably would not be given permission, but they also instinctively understood that social media was important to their mission and the future of their libraries. Today, the use of social media is standard in almost every higher education marketing and recruitment strategy nationwide, perhaps even globally.

The mass media and their reaction to social media also deserve a mention. They made things very hard for the early adopters. In the early years, the media's coverage of social networking was mostly fear-based and paranoid. In 2006 and 2007, they had every parent across America convinced that social networking would result in a worst-case scenario. Professionals thought that it was silly and reserved for the young. Psychologists thought that it would destroy human relationships. To be an early adopter of social networking required fortitude and conviction in those years. My guess is that the mass media were initially threatened. The Internet and blogging had already dealt a blow to their circulation and viewing numbers, and social networking had the possibility to further that downward trend. Fortunately, the media began to realize that it was wise for them to embrace social networking rather than continue to be critical outsiders. Most print, broadcast, and radio media outlets now utilize social media daily, and they have become an important voice on social networking sites. Indeed, the decision to participate rather than shun could very well turn out be their salvation.

And that leads to an important conclusion of this introduction. The media and institutions of higher education learned the hard way that early adoption is a wise and advantageous strategy in and of itself, and they are not making the same mistake with mobile technology. They have begun to pioneer the use of mobile websites, group texting, and smartphone and tablet apps. The business sector is enabling the rise of mobile technology through entrepreneurialism, and business marketers are also experimenting aggressively. Nonprofits, on the other hand, although they were early adopters of social media, have been very slow to adopt mobile technology. I believe the primary reason is that nonprofits think that implementing mobile campaigns is expensive and time-consuming. It was in 2009, but it's not anymore. A great number of cost-effective mobile technology tools that make mobile campaigns easy to implement and manage have been launched in recent years. This book will help you understand that and hopefully inspire your nonprofit to become a Web pioneer for social good once again.

WEB 1.0
THE STATIC WEB

WEBSITES, E-NEWSLETTERS, AND "DONATE NOW" CAMPAIGNS

IDEX's website hadn't been redesigned in 10 years and with the rise of social media and how dramatically the Web had changed since our last design, it was long overdue. Relaunched in 2010, our new website is a vast improvement, better tells the story of IDEX and our partners, and easily allows visitors to also connect with us on social media. It also has strategically placed donate and e-mail sign-up buttons to improve our online fundraising results— and the good news is that it has!

—Gillian Wilson, communications director, IDEX (International Development Exchange)

WEB 1.0 IS THE FOUNDATION FOR SUCCESSFUL ONLINE COMMUNICATIONS AND FUNDRAISING

Despite the buzz over social media in recent years, the Static Web and its tools remain the most powerful for your nonprofit. Even in this era of Facebook, Twitter, and LinkedIn, your nonprofit's website, e-newsletter, and "Donate Now" campaigns still need to be central in the planning and execution of your online communications and fundraising strategies. The return on investment (ROI) from using social media and mobile technology is directly connected to how well designed your website is, the size of your e-newsletter list, the quality of the content you provide, and the vendor you select to process your online donations. Now more than ever, nonprofits need to ensure that they are spending time and resources perfecting the implementation of their Web 1.0 campaigns.

The good news is that compared to 10 years ago, launching a well-designed website, e-newsletter, and Donate Now campaign is incredibly affordable. There are literally hundreds of low-cost vendors and free tools on the Web today that offer do-it-yourself technology with the design aesthetic of experienced professionals. Even if your nonprofit is on a very tight budget, with a little tech know-how and some training, you can have an exceptional Web 1.0 presence. That said, for your nonprofit to be effective online, you must to be willing to invest a bare-bones minimum of $2,500 a year in your Web 1.0 campaigns; $5,000 is much better, and $10,000 is more realistic. Cut your print budget if you have to. You will eventually do so anyway, and to be successful online, it's crucial that you place your website, your e-newsletter, and your Donate Now campaigns at the very top of your list of priorities. Your Web 1.0 campaigns need to make a strong first impression if supporters, especially online donors, are to take your nonprofit seriously.

FIVE MUST-HAVE CHARACTERISTICS OF A NONPROFIT WEBSITE

The size of your nonprofit's website in terms of the number of pages will vary according to its purpose, but it is increasingly true that websites need not serve as the primary content hub for your nonprofit's brand. Rather, your online brand and messages will be spread out among many channels (blogging, Facebook, Twitter, mobile, and so on) to reach supporters of all ages and backgrounds. There is no one-size-fits-all anymore in Web communications. Your supporters now use a wide variety of communication channels to access your nonprofit online, and their primary preference is usually directly correlated to their generation. Millennials live and breathe social networking and increasingly prefer mobile. Gen X actively uses social networks and reads blogs. Matures browse websites and are increasingly donating online more often. All ages use e-mail. With the technology being constantly in flux, the one sure thing is that a website is not enough anymore to communicate your mission and programs; however, it is your starting point and the foundation of your online communications and fundraising campaigns.

Ironically, website design principles have come full circle over the last 10 years. The simple 5- to 20-page brochure website design aesthetics of the 1990s gave way in the 2000s to building multilayered websites with vast amounts of information about your nonprofit using elements of Flash and Java, and now, in the 2010s, websites are once again simple and streamlined, optimized for desktop, tablets, and mobile Web browsing. Simplicity in design, functionality, and content are the predominant website design principles of today, and this is likely to remain true for years to come as our society struggles to live with and manage information overload.

1. Easy-to-Use Content Management System

A content management system (CMS) is a software program that allows easy editing and maintenance of a website. There is an initial cost for setting up and designing a website using a CMS software program, but if the setup and design are done correctly, your nonprofit will not be dependent upon a third party to edit or add pages to your website. In the nonprofit sector, there are four free or low-cost, highly regarded CMSs: WordPress, Joomla!, Drupal, and eZ Publish. A quick Google search will reveal hundreds of WordPress, Joomla!, Drupal, and eZ Publish designers available for hire (fees range from $1,000 to $5,000), but you can also purchase WordPress, Joomla!, Drupal, and eZ Publish predesigned "themes" for as little as $50. With some technical training, a can-do attitude, and an approximate budget of $1,000 for a domain name, hosting, e-mail accounts, two to three hours of graphic design work, and a theme purchase, your nonprofit can launch a simple, professionally designed, modern website. Many themes also include the ability to incorporate a blog and other social media into the website. After the launch, all that is required is hosting fees and possibly additional graphic design work to keep your website looking fresh (approximately $500 to $1,000 per year). Ten years ago, the average cost for such a website would have been $25,000 or more. Today, such tools are affordable, extremely well built, and designed using Web 2.0 principles and aesthetics.

Another tool that is becoming increasing popular in the nonprofit sector is Squarespace.com. It's a one-stop, entirely Web-based, do-it-yourself website and blog publishing tool. You can completely customize the design or use preloaded templates (or a mixture of both), upload graphics, and insert a wide variety of widgets to add increased functionality to your website. Starting at $12 a month, including hosting, Squarespace is an exceptional value for small nonprofits that consistently struggle with maintaining a professional, current website.

If your nonprofit has a Web 1.0 budget of $5,000 or more per year, there are CMS vendors that specifically serve the nonprofit sector. Blackbaud and Convio are two of the best known. Both offer a CMS, e-newsletter publishing, online fundraising tools, a supporter and donor database, and customer service. Fees vary widely depending upon your organization's size and needs (Blackbaud starts at $10,000 annually), but if your nonprofit can afford it, these services will help you keep your online presence consistent and streamlined for easier management. If not, then, like most nonprofits, you'll need to use separate vendors for your website, e-newsletter, and online fundraising campaigns. Either way, rest assured that the Web is more affordable and easier to utilize today and that there are plenty of viable do-it-yourself options to choose from. That said, if your nonprofit is in the precarious position of being dependent upon a website designer to make edits or add pages to your website using a tool like Dreamweaver, then it is time to upgrade to a CMS. Today, the often frustrating and expensive model for website creation and management that ruled during the era of Web 1.0 is completely avoidable and unnecessary.

2. Good Writing

The ability to communicate ideas and calls to action in succinct two- to three-sentence paragraphs is an acquired skill. As a general rule, focus on one idea per paragraph in 100 words or fewer. Write with purpose and clarity, and strike out any words that hint of rambling, clichés, or fluff. At a time in our history when most ideas are expressed online in status updates and tweets, the ability to write with precision is required to keep readers engaged.

One of the best ways to improve your website writing skills is to increase your vocabulary. Often a concept that you want to communicate in five or six words can be narrowed to two or three with a quick search of the words on Thesaurus.com. If this doesn't do it, try Dictionary.com. And, of course, always check your spelling and grammar. Such mistakes are often overlooked on Facebook and Twitter, but rarely on websites.

3. Well-Designed Graphics and Photos

Well-designed graphics and powerful photos can speak volumes. Whereas text can easily overwhelm people or take too long to read for an ever-increasingly impatient Web audience, you can often communicate and inspire people instantaneously with strong visuals. Graphic design is likely to be your biggest expense when you are launching or redesigning your Web 1.0 campaigns, but it is a necessary one. As a starting point, and if you are on a limited budget, hire a designer to create one powerful banner and use it for the top of your website, your blog, and your e-newsletter. From there, if you have more funds to spend, create additional banners for secondary pages on your website, similar in style but varied in colors and images. Next in priority are custom-designed "Donate Now" and "Subscribe" buttons, social media icons, text-to-give and text-to-subscribe pitches, and event promotion graphics. All graphics should be consistent in look and feel, and ideally should be designed by the same person or firm.

Also, if you don't have a large digital photo library, buy a digital camera and start to build one. You will need a wide variety of images to choose from to successfully implement your Web 1.0, Web 2.0, and Web 3.0 campaigns. You can legally download free images from Creative Commons, Flickr, and Google Images, or, when necessary, you can purchase copyrighted photos and graphics from paid subscription services.

4. Simple, Consistent Navigation

Your website navigation should be consistent throughout the site. Ideally, every page of your website should have primary navigation across the top of the page, with access to secondary pages in the left or right margin. All pages should be the same dimensions so that the click-through process is swift and consistent. Today's Web users expect professional polish and have almost zero tolerance for getting lost inside your site as a result of poor navigation.

5. A Dot.org Website Address

The website suffix "org" is an abbreviation for "organization," and having one is a long-standing best practice for nonprofit websites. Such an address can be purchased for as little as $10 a year at domain name registration services like Register.com or Network Solutions. Purchasing a dot.org domain name also allows your non-profit to set up e-mail accounts with your dot.org domain name. Under no circumstances should your nonprofit be using a third-party e-mail domain name for communication with your support-ers, such as Gmail.com. Even if your nonprofit uses Gmail as its primary e-mail client, you can still configure Gmail to send and receive your e-mails with dot.org domain name e-mail accounts. Purchasing the domain name, the website hosting package, and the e-mail account service usually costs no more than $150 per year. These are mandatory expenses for every nonprofit that wants to convey a professional website and e-mail strategy. No excuses. Online donors and supporters now expect this baseline of expertise in online communications.

ELEVEN WEBSITE DESIGN
BEST PRACTICES FOR NONPROFITS

The rise of social media and mobile technology has changed the way people process information. The 24/7 news cycle is overwhelming to many people. Websites that are burdened with too much text or too many images without consistency in size and color scheme can immediately lead to an exit response. Whether we like it or not, infor-mation overload is a part of our culture now, and the design and tone of your nonprofit's website need to take this shift in communication seriously and present your website accordingly. Simplicity is key.

Your supporters also now expect a more social experience from your website. It's crucial that your social media and mobile technol-ogy campaigns are integrated into your website. You may need to completely start over with your website, or you may simply need to tweak your current design, but make no mistake: the general principles and design aesthetics that ruled during the era of Web 1.0 are no longer applicable.

1. Have a Simple, Visually Powerful Web 2.0 Home Page Design

The home page of today should have large, powerful images and minimal text. Navigation should be bold, bright, and obvious. The upper right-hand corner is the most valuable section of your website—use it to plug your e-newsletter and group text messaging campaigns, Donate Now functionality, and social networking communities. Icons and buttons have strong appeal and impact in Web 2.0 design and result in more clicks than text links. Overall, avoid clutter. Too much text and multiple links to choose from can easily overwhelm readers to the point where more than anything they just want to leave your website.

2. Have a Consistent Design throughout All Secondary Navigation and Content Pages

A good CMS will take care of this for you. All content pages should be the same size and should be consistent in their layout and color scheme. Use the Arial, Times New Roman, Verdana, or Georgia font. Text should be black, the background of content pages should be white, and the color of the links should be coordinated with the website's color scheme. In general, limit the use of colors to three or four. Images should be consistent in size and resolution and should be placed in the same location on every page. Repetition is key.

3. Format Text for Easy Reading

Write for Web 2.0! Limit paragraphs to two to four sentences, with line breaks between paragraphs. Use bold for headlines. Keep bullet-pointed content short. Most important, avoid long pages that require excessive scrolling.

4. Limit the Layout to Two Columns

Web 1.0 websites tried to pack in as much content as possible through a three- and sometimes four-column design structure. No longer! Today, a good design structure for a website will have two columns. One column will take up two-thirds of the page layout (or a little more) for content stories, and the other third is for secondary navigation and graphics for special campaigns.

5. Write Page Titles That Increase Your Search Engine Optimization

Meta tags have been abused by so many shifty search engine optimization (SEO) specialists over the past 10 years that search engines are increasingly giving higher priority to page titles to generate their search results. Therefore, every page of your website should have a unique title. Make sure your home page has your organization's name and tagline. Secondary pages should have your organization's name and a unique title for each page. If you use your website to publish news stories or press releases, make sure that the titles of the press releases and articles include words and phrases that people who may be interested in your mission and programs are likely to type into Google, Bing, or Yahoo!. Meta tags are still relevant, but fresh content and page titles are increasingly dominating search results.

6. Subscribe to E-newsletter and Group Text Messaging Functionality

The ability to subscribe to your nonprofit's e-newsletter and group text messaging campaigns should be featured prominently on every page of your website. "Subscribe" buttons should be embedded on your home page (ideally in the upper right-hand corner), and also on every secondary page within your website. Also, it's important that you keep the subscription process as simple as possible. Don't require a snail mail address or a username and password to subscribe, and if you must ask for the person's name in order to personalize your campaign, make only the first name a mandatory field. If your nonprofit requires more than two or three pieces of information to subscribe to your e-newsletter, you will lose many potential subscribers. Finally, make it mandatory that the subscriber enter his zip code only if your organization plans on doing advocacy campaigns via e-mail or group text messaging.

7. Include Social Media Icons or Graphics

A good number of your Facebook fans, Twitter followers, and Flickr, YouTube, and Foursquare friends will come directly from clicks on social media icons placed on your website alongside "Follow Us" pitches. There are hundreds of free social media icon sets accessible through Google searches, but if you have access to a good graphic designer, consider getting a set custom-designed that matches the branding of your website.

8. Have a "Donate Now" Button on Every Page

A large, colorful "Donate Now" button should be featured on your home page and on every secondary page thereafter. Ideally, the button should be in close proximity to your social media icons and "Subscribe" buttons, and should be custom-designed to match your website's branding. The easiest way to integrate Donate Now, Subscribe, and Follow Us pitches into all pages on your website is to include them in your top or sidebar navigation. Make sure that your "Donate Now" button links directly to a page that asks for contact and credit card information, not to a general "Support Us" page. Online donors are often impulsive and don't want to navigate through numerous pages and fundraising requests to make a donation. Make the process as effortless and clutter-free as possible.

9. Integrate Social Media into Secondary Pages

Articles and information pages that are text-only tend to overwhelm visitors. An embedded video or slideshow can add value to your text if it is relevant and well produced. Videos and photos help tell your organization's story better, and often inspire donors and supporters to give and take action in a way that text by itself simply cannot.

10. Use Third-Party Widgets Only if They Add Value

The Web has become overrun with widgets! Some are useful and well designed (such as the Facebook Like Box and the Twitter Profile Widget), but the majority add clutter and inconsistency to your website. Though you may be tempted to embrace widgets because of their simplicity of use and the shiny new tool factor, choose wisely and with caution. Too many widgets of various sizes and colors will confuse your visitors as to what they are supposed to focus on or do and most likely will send them the unintentional message that your website is managed by an amateur. As a general rule of thumb, keep widgets off your home page.

11. Host Your Blog Inside Your Website

Depending upon your budget and the CMS you use for your website, the best way to optimize your online brand and SEO is to host your blog inside your nonprofit's website, such as nrdc.org/blog. The obvious benefit is that every time you publish and then promote a blog post on a social networking site or in your e-newsletter, the blog post drives traffic to your website. Less obvious, but just as important, the more content you publish under your URL (www.nrdc.org, for example), the higher your nonprofit will rank in search engine results, since Google, Bing, and Yahoo! are increasingly giving fresh blog content priority over static Web pages. The power of blogging for SEO should not be underestimated.

THE IMPORTANCE OF THE E-NEWSLETTER

E-mail is not dead. Not having an e-newsletter for your nonprofit is folly. Your e-newsletter is the number one force driving traffic to your website, your blog, your "Donate Now" landing page, and your social networking profiles. It's true that e-newsletter open rates are dropping on average 1 percent per year, and no doubt e-mail will be eulogized eventually, but for now, e-mail is still queen. In fact, in a report released in late 2010 by the Pew Research Center's Internet & American Life Project, e-mail is the only tool used by large numbers of people from all generations—from Millennials (18–33) to the G.I. Generation (74+). In the era of the Social Web, the e-newsletter subscription rate in the nonprofit sector is actually growing—especially for small nonprofits, which for the first time have the means to access thousands of potential new subscribers through social networking sites.

That said, the term *e-newsletter* is a bit of a misnomer. Information overload and the rise of social media have changed the way individuals consume e-mail content. The Web 1.0 model of using e-mail to publish an electronic version of your print newsletter is no longer a best practice. Most people don't want to read your e-newsletter that deeply anymore, particularly Gen Y and Millennials. They want to be able to scan your e-newsletter quickly for the primary call to action or news story, and then quickly move on. Today, it's better to think of your e-newsletter as an "e-bulletin" that is sent out to remind your supporters that your nonprofit is making progress in its mission and programs and that you need their continued support.

HOW TO LAUNCH AN E-NEWSLETTER

The easiest, most productive way to launch and maintain an e-newsletter is to use a hosted e-mail marketing service such as iContact, MailChimp, Constant Contact, VerticalResponse, or EmailNow from Network for Good. Monthly fees range from $15 to $150, depending on your list size ($75 a month is the average for a 10,000-member list). This is an absolutely mandatory expense for nonprofits! Hosted e-mail marketing services provide an easy-to-use Web-based database that enables automatic subscribe and unsubscribe functionality, follows CAN-SPAM laws, and provides useful open and click-through rate statistics that are necessary to maintain a successful e-newsletter campaign.

Under no circumstances should your nonprofit be publishing e-newsletters via BCC using an e-mail client like Gmail or Outlook. That method is antiquated and counterproductive, but it is still shockingly common among small nonprofits. Most of those e-mails go straight into spam folders, require manual contact list management, and are usually poorly designed. Most online donors and supporters expect a much more polished and professional e-newsletter than a do-it-yourself-via-BCC e-newsletter can offer.

Finally, a 20 percent open rate is considered average for the nonprofit sector. Set that as your baseline for success, and then test and experiment to achieve a rate of 25 to 35 percent. It is worth noting that nonprofits that send out one or two e-newsletters a month tend to have higher open rates than those that e-mail more frequently. You'll have to find the right balance over time in terms of the number of e-newsletters to send per month, but if your rate drops below 20 percent, then adjust your frequency accordingly.

ELEVEN E-NEWSLETTER BEST PRACTICES FOR NONPROFITS

The nonprofit sector has more than 10 years of experience in publishing e-newsletters. There are many proven best practices and case studies of what works and what doesn't. However, with the rise of social media and mobile technology, many of those best practices and case studies have been rendered irrelevant. As in most forms of communication these days, best practices are in a constant state of flux. The best practices listed here may be different or even irrelevant in a few years, but for now, early adopters and forward thinkers are transforming the way we use e-mail for social good.

1. Keep Your E-newsletter Design Simple

Five years ago, three-column e-newsletters loaded with graphics and photos and featuring four or five stories were the standard best practice. Not anymore. People are inundated with information and images all day long from a variety of sources, and too much content can be both a visual and a mental distraction. If you want to get the attention of your readers, keep your e-newsletter design simple. Make it a single column, and use black text on a white background for the body content. You should use one color for the background image (behind the body content), not patterns or graphics, and have a simple header image at the top that includes your logo and tagline. Oceana was a pioneer in utilizing e-newsletters, and its current design is a great example of how to successfully design an e-newsletter in the era of the Social Web.

2. Publish E-newsletters That Are 500 Words or Less

Your subscribers are busy people. They need to be able to digest the subject of your e-newsletter in 5 to 15 seconds. Limit the content to one or two news items or organizational updates that clearly let them see what they need to do or click if they are to take action, learn more, make a donation, RSVP, or do something else. As when formatting the text on your website, keep paragraphs short with line breaks in between. Color your links to make them stand out. Use bold headlines to make your e-newsletter easy to skim. If you need more than 500 words, then link to an article on your website or a blog where subscribers can "Read More." Also, in some cases you'll want to use a "P.S." to repeat and accentuate the request to take action.

3. Add a "Donate Now" Button and Social Media Icons

The vast majority of your online donations and your new friends, followers, and fans will come from your e-newsletter. That's why nonprofits with large e-newsletter lists are consistently able to raise the most money online and tend to have the largest communities on social networking sites. You don't need to make a direct request in every issue of your e-newsletter, but you should have your "Donate Now" button and social networking icons designed into your e-newsletter template. Most nonprofits put the button and icons along the bottom of their e-newsletter, but some incorporate them into the banner across the top of their e-newsletter.

4. Make It Personal

Your e-newsletter should use language that makes your subscribers feel that they are a part of your organization. Use words like "we/us/together" and "I" statements. Also, some nonprofits may choose to have their e-newsletter arrive in people's inboxes from a person rather than just the nonprofit name, such as "Mark @ Save Darfur Coalition" or "Mark, Save Darfur Coalition." Of course, if you do this, you should also have an individual sign-off on the e-newsletter. If your nonprofit has a strong leader or personality, experiment with having her as the sender of occasional e-newsletters and see if it improves your open rates.

5. Make It Social

A relatively new perk that most hosted e-mail marketing service providers have added is the ability to make your e-newsletters easily shareable on social networking sites. Once you are logged into your dashboard, locate the functionality to make your content shareable and turn it on. Subscribers can then easily share your e-newsletters on Twitter, Facebook, and other social media with just a click or two.

6. Use Screenshots for Videos and Slideshows

Currently there is no way to upload a video to a hosted e-newsletter, and embedded code for videos and slideshows is not yet standard across all platforms, but inserting a screenshot of your video(s) or slideshow(s) into your e-newsletter can significantly increase your click-through rates. People like to be entertained and told a story though video and digital photography. To take a screenshot, simply click and hold down "CTRL" and "ALT" simultaneously, then > "PRNTSCR" on your PC ("Command > Shift > 3" on Mac computers). That essentially takes a snapshot of your computer screen, such as a YouTube Channel or Flickr slideshow, that you can then paste into your chosen photo editing software. Crop appropriately and then insert the image into your e-newsletter. Ideally, the image should link to a page in your website or blog where you have the video or slideshow embedded, but linking it directly to your YouTube Channel or Flickr account is a good practice as well.

7. Send Test Versions of Your E-newsletters to Multiple E-mail Platforms

Another reason to keep your e-newsletter template design as simple as possible is that e-newsletters often look different in Gmail, Outlook, Yahoo!, Hotmail, and other platforms. The less fancy your formatting and design, the more likely it is that your e-newsletter will look the same in various e-mail clients. While this may be frustrating and take a little more time to manage, you should sign up for numerous e-mail accounts and review your design in each e-mail platform to make sure that there is consistency and there are no glaring design mistakes. Ideally, you should do this with every issue. Supporters are much less forgiving of mistakes in Web 1.0 communications than they are in Web 2.0 communications.

8. Create a "Thank You for Subscribing" E-mail That Pitches Your Website, Blog, and Social Networking Communities

Most hosted e-newsletter services allow you to create follow-up e-mails that are automatically sent to new subscribers. This is the first e-mail that your subscribers will receive from your nonprofit, so make sure that the design is good, that the tone is gracious and friendly, and that it includes a direct request that the subscriber visit your website and blog, like you on Facebook, follow you on Twitter, and so on. However, don't ask for a donation! There's plenty of time for that later. Hosted e-mail services also allow you to create "Thank You for Subscribing" landing pages. Be sure to pitch your website, blog, and social networking communities there as well.

9. Keep Subject Lines Short and Varied

Over the years, hundreds of blog posts and articles have been written about what makes a good subject line for your e-newsletter, and what we've discovered is that short subject lines (60 characters or fewer) tend to result in the highest open rates. That said, a boring, short subject line like "Volume 34, Issue 16" won't produce great results. Creative subject lines that pique curiosity and vary from issue to issue are the magic formula for higher open rates.

10. Send One to Three E-newsletters per Month and up to Six Fundraising Appeals per Year

A lot of nonprofits get overzealous in their e-mail marketing, sending e-newsletters once or twice a week. For most nonprofits, that's just too much. At that rate, the law of diminishing returns kicks in almost immediately. People start to ignore your e-mails or, worse, unsubscribe. On average, send one to three e-newsletters per month and monitor your open and unsubscribe rates. There will always be unsubscribes, but if they go above 0.5 percent, then lower your frequency of e-newsletters sent. If your nonprofit engages in advocacy or hosts many events, then you can experiment with four or five per month, but it's important to keep in mind that many people feel inundated with e-mail these days. You want to be well received in their inbox, not considered an annoyance.

In addition to the one to three e-newsletters per month, send up to six fundraising appeals per year. Since most donors give in November and December, schedule at least three of these appeals for the last two months of the year. These appeals should clearly explain why and how to donate and communicate a sense of urgency. Again, you should have a "Donate Now" button in every edition of your e-newsletter and do more subtle requests throughout the year, but e-newsletters containing only a fundraising appeal should be sent with intention and strategy.

11. Don't Send Your E-newsletter like Clockwork

Mix it up! Don't always send your e-newsletter on Mondays at 10 a.m. Try Tuesday afternoons, Thursday mornings, and occasionally a week-end edition. The Web ebbs and flows, and so should your e-newsletter schedule. It's almost impossible to predict what day and time works best for e-newsletters because it is constantly changing depending on current events, holidays, and nonprofits following en masse a best-day-and-time strategy proclaimed by a well-read blog or case study. Keep your e-newsletter schedule sporadic and unpredictable. Once it becomes predictable, your open rate will begin to decline.

FIVE WAYS TO BUILD YOUR E-NEWSLETTER LIST

According to the 2011 *Convio Online Nonprofit Benchmark Study*, the average value of an e-mail address in the nonprofit sector is $12.48 in online donations. Nonprofits that have been utilizing e-newsletters for years probably already have a working knowledge of why and how to build their lists and regularly ask donors, supporters, and volunteers for their e-mail addresses. If you are new to publishing e-newsletters, building your list should be one of your top priorities. When you fol-low the five suggestions given here, the size of your list and your online donations will grow steadily over time.

For your first edition, you can include past donors, event atten-dees, and staff members and volunteers in your e-newsletter list as long as you clearly state in that first edition that they have been added to the list because they have been supporters of your organization in the past. After that, you will have to follow a strict opt-in only policy to build your list. You can't just add people to your list because you think they would like to receive your e-newsletter. For that first edition, you can bend the rules a bit, but only for people who have clearly supported your organization in the past. There is a proper etiquette to follow when building your lists, and subscribing people without their permission definitely breaks the rules.

1. Add Subscribe Functionality to Your Website and Your Blog

In addition to including your "Subscribe" button or a link to your website, make sure you feature a "Subscribe" button on your blog as well. Since blogs tend to be more personal, and often more interesting, than static website content, the number of people who subscribe to your e-newsletter from your blog will sometimes be much higher than the number who do on your website.

All hosted e-newsletter services offer sign-up boxes that can be added to your website or blog simply by copying and pasting a small piece of HTML code. They also provide customizable landing pages if you prefer to feature a "Subscribe" button or link. Keep your pitch to subscribe brief, and let people know that you respect their privacy by mentioning that you will not buy, sell, or trade their e-mail addresses (unless you plan on doing so; many nonprofits do).

2. Ask Supporters to Subscribe via Status Updates and Tweets

Once or twice a month, send out tweets or status updates asking people to sign up to receive your e-newsletter. Always include a link to your "Subscribe" landing page. This strategy works best if you mention a rapidly approaching deadline, such as

> Working on the next edition of our e-newsletter. Scheduled to be sent tomorrow! To receive a copy, please subscribe: http://bit.ly/yoursubscribelink.

3. Pitch Your E-newsletter in All Print Materials

Make sure that all donation forms in your print newsletter and funding appeals have an e-mail field. You can then manually add those new e-mail addresses to the database inside your chosen hosted e-newsletter service. Also, in the "Learn More" or "Get Involved" sections of your print materials, let people know that they can subscribe to your e-newsletter by visiting your website.

4. Use Sign-up Sheets at Events

Whether you're hosting your annual gala or your monthly open house, always have a sign-up sheet for your e-newsletter. It's a best practice never to put out an empty sign-up sheet. Sign up your mother or your boyfriend or your wife to get the sign-ups rolling. It's just a phenomenon of human nature that most people will pass by an empty sign-up sheet, but will sign on eagerly if they see others doing the same.

5. Create Online E-mail Petitions

Social good sites like Change.org and Care2.com allow nonprofits to create Web-based e-mail petitions, a practice better known as e-advocacy. Supporters sign on to an e-mail petition, which results in a politician receiving an e-mail asking him to support certain legislation or a corporation receiving one asking it to change its business practices. A lot of people have termed e-advocacy "slacktivism" and claim that it results in a false sense of doing social good, but little actions can result in big changes over time. In terms of building your list, you can purchase the e-mail addresses of the people who opt-in and sign your e-mail petitions from Change.org or Care2.com (or other similar services) for a small fee. Most nonprofits cannot afford to purchase e-mail lists, but it is a common practice. Without a revenue model, social good sites that focus on e-advocacy cannot sustain themselves, and a donation-only revenue model has never worked.

There are also e-advocacy vendors that primarily serve the non-profit sector, such as Blackbaud, Convio, and DemocracyInAction. These vendors offer a wide variety of Web-based services, so if your nonprofit plans to engage heavily in e-advocacy, it's worth taking a few of their free Webinars to learn more about their suite of tools. Finally, e-advocacy is on the brink of going mobile. People will soon be signing petitions and participating in e-mail alerts directly from their mobile devices in massive numbers. Whatever service you decide to use to empower your e-advocacy campaigns, make sure that mobile advocacy is on its priority list.

THE POWER OF DONATE NOW CAMPAIGNS

Donate Now technology first became available to the nonprofit sector in 1999 thanks to JustGive.org and GroundSpring.org. The early adopters of "Donate Now" buttons in the nonprofit community were convinced that the technology would revolutionize philanthropy. They were just as passionate and bold as many of the early adopters of social media, and now mobile technology. Like the pioneers of Web 2.0 and Web 3.0, they had to maneuver resistance to change from the executive staff, calm the fears of donors who fretted that using a credit card online would result in hacked bank accounts, and consistently reinforce the idea that investing in Donate Now campaigns today would pay off down the road despite minimal results in terms of dollars raised in those early years.

It's a good thing that the early adopters remained diligent, because today Donate Now technology is finally starting to achieve its potential and is transforming fundraising and giving. Ironically, thanks to social media, people and nonprofits are connecting online in ways that were never imagined 10 years ago, and as a result online giving is growing consistently and rapidly with each passing year.

THE IMPORTANCE OF SELECTING THE RIGHT DONATE NOW VENDOR

The most important decision your nonprofit will make when executing and maintaining your online fundraising strategy will be what vendor you select to empower your Donate Now campaigns. Tragically, many nonprofits try to save pennies when selecting a vendor for their "Donate Now" button and landing page, and as a result, they end up turning away many potential online donors. Now more than ever, nonprofits should be investing time and financial resources in their Donate Now campaigns.

On average, nonprofits should expect to pay 3 to 5 percent in processing fees. That's the industry standard and the price you have to pay to raise funds successfully online. Unfortunately, many nonprofits try to save 0.5 percent or less and opt to use vendors that do not offer custom branding for "Donate Now" landing pages, recurring donations, or gift donation capability, costing them much more in donations that never were because of a poor choice in vendor selection. On top of processing fees, a branded "Donate Now" landing page embedded in your website is going to run your organization an average of $50 a month. Make every attempt possible to include these funds in your annual budget because if you do not have a branded "Donate Now" landing page inside your website, you've probably lost $600 or more a year in online donations.

Today there are well over 100 Donate Now vendors available to the nonprofit sector. You can easily be overwhelmed by the number of choices and the differences in functionality offered by each. Here are the vendors that were recommended most often by nonprofits in research conducted for this book through Twitter polls and LinkedIn discussions, with highlights of the services that they offer. For additional information, many of these vendors offer free Webinars that can be viewed by visiting their websites. Again, this is one of the most important decisions you will make for your nonprofit, so choose wisely.

1. Network for Good

As the largest processor of online donations in the United States, Network for Good offers generic "Donate Now" landing pages for more than 1 million nonprofits through its giving portal as well as a premium Donate Now service. That said, if your nonprofit is a legal 501(c)(3) and thus is listed in the GuideStar database, then your nonprofit already has a generic "Donate Now" page on NetworkforGood .org. You can simply link to this page, known as the vendor's basic service, directly from your website. The donation processing fee is 5 percent. You get a monthly donor report, recurring donation capability, automatic e-mail receipts for donors, online donation tracking, and the ability to have your funds electronically transferred each month. The biggest drawbacks to the basic service are that donors can opt out of providing you with contact information, you cannot customize the "Donate Now" landing page to match your nonprofit's branding, and there is no capability to offer gift donations. This is a fine option if you are on a $0 budget, but just realize that you will lose some donors by sending them to the Network for Good website, where they have to create an account to give, and you will lose precious donor contact information for those who choose to give anonymously.

The premium service costs $50 a month and charges a 3 percent donation processing fee. The service provides customizable "Donate Now" landing pages that can be embedded in your website, donor contact information, recurring giving and gift donation capabilities, donation receipts, and comprehensive donation tracking and reporting tools. Network for Good reports that the average return for every $1 spent by a nonprofit using its premium service results in $25 raised in online donations. As mentioned earlier, this $600 in annual fees is the best investment your nonprofit could be making right now to increase your online fundraising, and, currently, Network for Good offers the best premium service at the most affordable price.

2. JustGive.org

Like Network for Good, JustGive.org is also a portal empowered by GuideStar, where your nonprofit most likely already has a "Donate Now" page that is almost identical to Network for Good's basic service. The big difference is that JustGive.org's basic service charges only 3 percent and does allow gift donations. If you are on a $0 budget, JustGive.org is a better option. The biggest drawback is that donors have to create an account on JustGive.org to donate. It's as simple as creating a password, but for some online donors, that's enough to turn them away.

3. Blackbaud, Convio, and DemocracyInAction

There is no shortage of companies that offer comprehensive Web-based communication and fundraising services for your nonprofit, but Blackbaud, Convio, and DemocracyInAction are the ones that were most highly recommended by nonprofits for this book (honorable mentions include Wild Apricot, Sage Nonprofit Solutions, DonorPerfect, Qgiv, and Click & Pledge). In general, your nonprofit needs to sign up for a suite of tools—website CMS, e-newsletter, Donate Now, donor database, e-advocacy, peer-to-peer fundraising, event management, and so on—to become a client. Again, fees vary widely depending upon your organization's size and needs, and it would be wise to get numerous price quotes. That said, over the long run, having all your Web-based communications and fundraising efforts housed with one vendor ensures time efficiency, consistency in implementation, and probably higher ROI.

What about PayPal?

Many nonprofits use PayPal to process their online donations because PayPal's fees are low compared to those of most other Donate Now vendors. Unfortunately, this decision could be costing these nonprofits thousands of dollars per year in lost revenue because some online donors simply refuse to donate through PayPal. Past security issues on PayPal and charity scams make some online donors nervous. PayPal doesn't offer branding options for "Donate Now" landing pages, and according to Network for Good, donors that do give through generic landing pages like those offered by PayPal (and Google Checkout) are 67 percent less likely to donate again. Also, donors often experience technical issues when giving through PayPal. Many think that they have to create a PayPal account to make a donation, which turns away some donors, and others may already have their e-mail address in PayPal's system from a past transaction and thus will sometimes encounter obstacles when attempting to make the donation.

The brutal truth is that the decision to use PayPal sends the message to many donors that you are a small-time organization. If you are happy with that assessment, then by all means use PayPal, but if you want to reach all online donors, then you need to stop trying to save pennies and invest in another Donate Now vendor. PayPal is great for business and e-commerce, but it does not provide some key technological features that are necessary if you are to implement successful Donate Now campaigns.

There are two exceptions when it comes to PayPal and the nonprofit sector. The first is that nonprofits located in the developing world have extremely limited options for fundraising online because they cannot be listed in any of the GuideStar databases (United States, United Kingdom, Canada, Australia, and, most recently, Israel), and thus verified online as legitimate nonprofits. Most donors who give to nonprofits in developing nations know this and are willing to give through PayPal. Second, PayPal is innovating mobile payments. Individuals can send your nonprofit funds using PayPal's mobile website or smartphone apps, one of which utilizes "bump" technology (literally bumping phones to make cash transactions). If your nonprofit wants to accept payments on your smartphone anywhere, anytime, then PayPal could be a good choice for your nonprofit. That said, mobile payment technology is exploding, and vendors that specifically serve the nonprofit sector may be a better choice.

What Vendors Are Available to Nonprofits outside the United States?

Again, PayPal is a good choice for nonprofits in the developing world. There is also Ammado.com, based in Ireland. It processes donations in more than 75 currencies for nonprofits all over the world. It offers a suite of tools ranging from giving widgets and fundraising circles to online petitions. Fees range from 5 to 7.5 percent. GlobalGiving.org is another option. You have to apply to get a "project" by your nonprofit listed on its site, but if you are approved, the donations are funneled through its U.S.-based foundation, so donations are tax-deductible for donors in the United States. Unfortunately, it looks as though GlobalGiving accepts only a small number of "partners," most likely because of capacity issues. Technically and financially, it's very difficult to process donations for nonprofits that cannot be listed in GuideStar databases. Both Ammado and GlobalGiving have to manage their own due diligence systems, which is costly and time-consuming.

Finally, in Canada, there is CanadaHelps.org. FirstGiving.org and VirginMoneyGiving.org are popular in the U.K., IsraelGives.org is available in Israel, GiveIndia.org in India, and for nonprofits in Australia, there are GiveNow.com.au and Donations.com.au. A simple Google search with "[your country] + online fundraising resources" generally tends to pull up results of the best online fundraising options for your nonprofit no matter what your global location.

FIVE MUST-HAVE CHARACTERISTICS OF A "DONATE NOW" LANDING PAGE

A "Donate Now" landing page is the page on your website where donors enter their credit card information. Online donors arrive on this page by directly clicking a "Donate Now" button on your website or blog, or from a status update or tweet. The importance of this page should not be underestimated. It will make or break your online fundraising campaigns.

1. It Has Your Organization's Branding

Your "Donate Now" landing page should have the branding of your website, not PayPal or Google's branding! If you want to maximize your online donations, your "Donate Now" landing page needs to be embedded within your website, not hosted on a third-party website. Online donors are finicky and expect the utmost professionalism in online giving.

2. There Is an Opt-in Option for an E-newsletter

Most "Donate Now" landing pages have an e-mail address field in order to mail the donor a receipt. Make sure you also give donors the ability to check or uncheck a box (if automatic opt-in is the default setting) to subscribe to your e-newsletter near the e-mail address field. The e-mail addresses are then provided to the nonprofit, usually by means of monthly donor reports provided by your Donate Now vendor. Under no circumstances should you be using a vendor that does not provide your nonprofit with the opted-in contact information of your donors! Your e-newsletter is your most important tool to get your supporters to donate again.

3. It Has the Option to Give Monthly or Quarterly

On average, 10 percent of your online donors will sign up to automatically donate a set amount at regular intervals, usually monthly. These are funds that your nonprofit can consistently count on, and the opt-out rate is minimal. Most often, the ability to sign up for recurring donations simply requires checking a box and then selecting monthly, quarterly, or annually from a pop-down menu located just below the donation amount field on your "Donate Now" landing page. Using a vendor that does not allow recurring donations can cost your nonprofit thousands of dollars in lost revenue each year.

4. It Has the Option to Give in Someone Else's Name

Gift donations are becoming increasingly popular for birthdays, weddings, and holidays. Your vendor should offer the capability to make a donation in someone else's name directly from the "Donate Now" landing page. Donors then enter the e-mail address of the gift recipient and a brief message, and a gift notification is then e-mailed to the gift recipient.

5. It Is Designed for Expediency

The donation process should begin and end on your "Donate Now" landing page! Don't require multiple steps and pages to complete a donation. Keep it as simple as possible, and require only fields that are absolutely necessary to process a donation. Nothing is more annoying to busy online donors than a seemingly tedious online donation process.

ELEVEN DONATE NOW BEST PRACTICES FOR NONPROFITS

Pundits and bloggers in the nonprofit sector often lament the inability of social media to raise money for nonprofits. It's true that Web 2.0 widgets and apps have yet to raise large amounts in online dollars for most nonprofits, but that doesn't mean that social media is not resulting in large amounts of dollars raised online. There is no denying that the rise in online giving over the last few years directly correlates with the rise of social media. While it's impossible to track these donations unless you poll your online donors, the more your nonprofit utilizes social media to build your online brand and your e-newsletter list, the more likely potential online donors are to discover your nonprofit—and your nonprofit's "Donate Now" landing page.

1. Make Sure Your Nonprofit's Information in GuideStar Is Current

GuideStar.org is an online database of verified legal nonprofits that helps empower online fundraising campaigns for more than a million IRS-recognized nonprofits. As mentioned earlier, both Network for Good and JustGive.org use GuideStar to empower their giving portals as well as the online donation processing technology of their partners, such as Facebook Causes, Crowdrise, and Jumo. If your nonprofit is a legal 501(c)(3), then it has a profile in the GuideStar database, and consequently on Network for Good, JustGive.org, Facebook Causes, Crowdrise, and Jumo as well. It's important that you understand that if anyone donates to your nonprofit on any of these sites, the funds are mailed to the contact information your nonprofit has in GuideStar. Therefore, it's crucial that you update your GuideStar "Nonprofit Report" at least once a year. The process can be a little tedious, but it's necessary. If your address, nonprofit name, or mission is incorrect, then it's also incorrect on Network for Good and JustGive.org's giving portals and their partner sites. Increasingly, online donors are giving through portals and social networking sites, so you must make sure that your nonprofit is properly listed in GuideStar. On a final note, 501(c)(4) nonprofits do not appear in GuideStar because they are not included on the I.R.S. Business Master File (BMF), thus limiting their capacity to receive online donations from giving portals and social networking sites.

2. Monitor Your Charity Ratings and Reviews

Charity Navigator, also a nonprofit, is the best known and most respected independent charity rating service in the United States. Since it rates only the largest nonprofits in America, the odds are that if your nonprofit is listed on Charity Navigator, you'll know it. If it is not, you can request to be reviewed on the service's website. The Better Business Bureau also reviews national charities through its BBB Wise Giving Alliance program. If you are a national charity, you can also request to be reviewed on this website. GiveWell is another independent charity rating service, although it is much smaller. If your nonprofit is too small to be rated by these services, GuideStar and GreatNonprofits allow donors to review charities. It's a good idea to ask one or two of your key supporters to register with the sites and leave positive reviews.

3. Make Your "Donate Now" Button Stand Out from Your Website's Color Scheme

Studies have shown that "Donate Now" buttons that stand out from your website's overall color scheme result in more online dollars raised because online donors can't help but notice them. For example, if your website and your logo use two colors, pick a third color that coordinates well with them for your "Donate Now" button. Again, your "Donate Now" button should be visible and obvious on every page on your website. Design it into your website's template or navigation bar.

4. Keep Text and Graphics to a Bare Minimum on Your "Donate Now" Landing Page

Your "Donate Now" landing page should be as simple as possible and clutter-free. In just a few sentences, let donors know how their donations will support your mission and programs, and feature one powerful image or video that speaks to your work and progress. Be sure to mention that donations are tax-deductible. If you have positive ratings from Charity Navigator and the BBB, feature those graphics in the margins or along the bottom of the page. Neatly align all required fields for contact and credit card information, and double-space between fields and line breaks. Donors also appreciate simple pie charts that show how much is spent on programs vs. operations—as long the chart reflects that at least 75 percent of your budget goes directly to programs. Charity Navigator reports that 7 out 10 nonprofits in the United States do meet that minimum benchmark.

Also, space permitting, create and feature donation sound bites that highlight the impact of their donations. The American Society for the Prevention of Cruelty to Animals (ASPCA) highlights that a $36 donation will result in five dogs and cats getting vaccinated and spayed or neutered through its mobile clinic. The Second Harvest Food Bank promotes that a $50 gift provides 180 meals for hungry families, children, and seniors. International Development Exchange touts that a $100 donation initiates a rural women's organic farming collective in South

Africa. Donors want to feel that their contributions are powerful. It's worth noting that these pitches also work well in print materials.

5. Create Additional Pages for Other Ways to Give

In addition to a "Donate Now" landing page, you should also have a page on your website called "Support Us" or "Other Ways to Give" or "How You Can Help" where you neatly list information about becoming a member, monthly giving, gift donations, snail mail giving, workplace giving, planned giving, and so on. Rather than detailing all the ways to give on this page, simply summarize each giving option and then link to secondary pages that discuss the various ways to give in more detail. Also, if your nonprofit offers peer-to-peer fundraising campaigns, make sure that you also list "Become a Fundraiser" and link to a page that goes into more detail about creating fundraising pages and launching and maintaining a successful peer-to-peer fundraising campaign.

6. Include Your Mailing Address on Your "Donate Now" Landing Page for Check Donations

Often donors will click on your "Donate Now" button when they are looking for a mailing address to which to send in a check donation. Make sure that your mailing address is also featured either in the margin or at the bottom of your "Donate Now" landing page. It's also a good idea to confirm on your Contact Us page that the physical address listed is indeed where check donations can be mailed, or give another address if it is not. Major donors still predominantly give through checks, so make sure it's easy for them to find the mailing address for check donations on your website.

7. Launch a Sustainer Program

If your Donate Now vendor offers recurring donation capability, then launch a sustainer program. Create a page on your website, and perhaps even a print brochure to distribute at events, pitching the importance of becoming a sustainer, that is, a monthly or quarterly donor. The Humane Society brands its sustainers as "Humane Heroes." Mercy Corps asks supporters to become "Partners in Mercy." FINCA asks that you join its "Sustainer's Circle." Once you draft the content for your sustainer page, promote the program in print newsletters and funding appeals, on your blog, and to your social networking communities. For Web promotions, it's essential that you have a well-designed graphic that asks supporters to become sustainers. An initial investment of time and resources in creating and launching a sustainer program can result in tens of thousands of dollars raised in online donations over the long run.

8. Launch an Online Gift Donation Program

Similarly, if your Donate Now vendor offers the ability to donate in someone else's name, then launch a gift donation program. Again, create a Web page that explains how donors can make holiday and special occasion gift donations in the name of a friend, family, or work colleague directly on your "Donate Now" landing page. Explain clearly that they need to enter the gift recipient's name and e-mail address for the recipient to receive notification of the gift via e-mail. Highlight how the donation will help your nonprofit and foster social good. If possible, provide the option to snail mail a notification card to the gift recipient. Either buy cards in bulk or get your own designed. Hard copy notifications will increase the number of gift donations given, especially during the holiday season.

9. Ask Supporters to Donate Now via Status Updates and Tweets—Occasionally

One of the most common mistakes that nonprofits have made over the years in social media is asking their friends, followers, and fans to "Make a Donation!" before their communities were ready. Build the community first, and raise funds second. For the first few months, don't ask for any donations. Concentrate instead on finding your voice and nurturing your communities. If you rarely receive comments, thumbs ups, or retweets, then no doubt all those funding pleas are beginning to look desperate. Inspire first; ask later. On average, limit your fundraising appeals in status updates and tweets to twice a month. If your communities are engaged, then a few people will respond and give. That said, it's important to remember that you're much more likely to get online donations from friends, followers, and fans if you can entice them to subscribe to your e-newsletter.

10. Add a Facebook, Twitter, YouTube, or Other Pitch to Your "Thank You" Landing Page

After an online donor completes the online giving process, she should land on a "Thank You" page where she is of course thanked for her donation, but also informed that she can stay current on news and progress at your nonprofit by liking you on Facebook, following you on Twitter, subscribing to your YouTube Channel, and so on. Use either text and social media icons or Facebook and Twitter widgets, but not both. It's also a good idea to create an annual "Thank You" video from staff members and the communities you serve that can then be embedded in your "Thanks for Your Donation" landing page.

11. Send a Follow-up "Thank You" E-mail with Links to your Profiles on Social Media Sites

Similarly, add a Facebook, Twitter, YouTube, or other pitch to your "Thanks for Your Donation" follow-up e-mail. The primary purpose of this e-mail is to confirm the donation and provide donors with a record for tax purposes, but adding social media icons to the bottom of the e-mail with a one- or two-sentence pitch to "Connect to Us!" will help get your donors engaged with your nonprofit on social networking sites.

It's also important to ensure that this e-mail is sent to all donors who give to your nonprofit through giving portals. According to Network for Good, only half of the nonprofits that receive donations through its portal bother to follow up with a personalized "Thank You" e-mail. As a result, those donors tend to drop their giving over time. Portal giving now makes up 25 percent of all giving in the United States, so it is a source of revenue that cannot be ignored.

WHAT ABOUT PEER-TO-PEER FUNDRAISING?

Peer-to-peer fundraising is the concept of empowering your supporters to raise funds for your nonprofit. The best-known examples are walk/run/bowl/dance-a-thons. While this has been a popular fundraising model for decades, it's only in the last five years that peer-to-peer fundraising has become Web-enabled, primarily through "fundraising pages." You can opt to use third-party peer-to-peer fundraising tools like Razoo, Crowdrise, and FirstGiving to empower your fundraisers, or you can embed the functionality directly into your website if you are a client of Blackbaud, Convio, or DemocracyInAction. Either way, there's no shortage of available vendors to choose from, although they do vary in functionality.

When deciding what vendor to use, you want to make sure that its design is modern and that it offers basic custom branding. At the very least, you want your fundraisers to be promoting fundraising pages that feature your logo, your mission, and your website. The ability to have a custom banner across the top of your fundraising pages is a huge plus. People are much more likely to donate if they see your nonprofit's branding. Also, the vendor should provide widgets for your fundraisers and social networking integration and "Share" functionality. It's also worth noting that some nonprofits use peer-to-peer fundraising sites to empower their Donate Now campaigns. That said, it's wise to do so only if your nonprofit cannot afford a premium service that enables a custom-designed "Donate Now" landing page inside your website, if the donation processing fees are less than those of Network for Good and JustGive.org's basic service, and if you do not plan on launching sustainer or gift donation programs.

How much time and resources your nonprofit should invest in launching and maintaining peer-to-peer fundraising campaigns, however, does depend on your mission, your programs, and the commitment level of your supporters. If your nonprofit regularly hosts a-thons, then you should absolutely invest in peer-to-peer fundraising campaigns. Health organizations also tend to do well with peer-to-peer fundraising campaigns because often a close friend or family member suffers from an illness or, worse, dies from it, and supporters want to raise funds in his honor. Nonprofits that respond to natural disasters and time-sensitive crises can also be successful with peer-to-peer fundraising campaigns because so many social do-gooders want to do more to help than just donate during a time of crisis. They also want to raise funds.

Peer-to-peer fundraising is not for every nonprofit, but at the very least you should experiment by launching a peer-to-peer fundraising campaign that informs and enables your supporters to create fundraising pages to solicit online donations on behalf of your nonprofit in lieu of birthday or holiday gifts, or for wedding registries. Only a tiny fraction of your supporters will oblige, but one much-loved, passionate individual with lots of friends and family can easily raise thousands of dollars for your nonprofit. That said, the donation processing fees for peer-to-peer fundraising tools range from 3 to 10 percent, with Razoo being the most affordable. Using a peer-to-peer fundraising service that can be embedded directly inside your website may cost more up front, but it may save money in the long run. Research carefully and do your math before selecting a vendor!

Setting up your peer-to-peer fundraising campaign is the easy part; maintaining and inspiring your fundraisers is the greater challenge. Successful peer-to-peer fundraising does require that you

- *Clearly explain to your fundraisers how the tools work.* You should write a guide with useful fundraising tips and best practices. If you are a large organization with a lot of fundraisers, you should consider presenting regular Webinars on how to create a fundraising page and successfully raise donations online.

Mercy Corps has led very successful peer-to-peer fundraising campaigns through its MPower Projects (mercycorps.org/mpower). A great model for any nonprofit, Mercy Corps provides useful links to FAQ pages and prominently features contact information for any questions fundraisers might have.

- *Consistently thank and feature your top fundraisers.* Fundraisers appreciate and are further inspired by being recognized for their efforts. Ideally, you should manage a group e-mail list of your fundraisers to keep them engaged and informed, but occasional personal "Thank You" e-mails have a strong positive impact. Also, it's a good idea to feature "Fundraisers of the Month" on your blog. These blog posts can then also be shared on Facebook, on Twitter, and in your e-newsletters. They make featured fundraisers feel special and appreciated, and they can also inspire other supporters to become fundraisers themselves.

- *Host friendly competitions for those who raise the most funds.* A little competition never hurts! Perhaps tie your competitions in with the "Fundraiser of the Month" campaigns, or make them weekly, but offer top fundraisers incentives to raise funds. A T-shirt or coffee cup with your logo, a free membership in your nonprofit for a person of their choice, or free attendance at your next gala dinner all provide good incentives.

- *Encourage fundraisers to set realistic fundraising goals, such as $2,500.* One of the most common, though well-intentioned, mistakes made by fundraisers is setting very high fundraising goals, such as $20,000. This usually sets up a fundraiser for failure from the beginning and makes donors feel that their $25 or $50 donation is insignificant. You want to help fundraisers set goals that are attainable so that more people are inspired to give and so that the fundraisers experience success.

FINAL WORDS: UPGRADE NOW, OR BECOME OBSOLETE

If your nonprofit's website, e-newsletter, or Donate Now campaigns were implemented more than five years ago, odds are that they're outdated. With more than one million nonprofits in the United States alone and an increasingly tech-savvy donor base, only those nonprofits that invest time and resources in their Web 1.0 campaigns today will continue to succeed tomorrow. Add to that the fact that social media has enabled tens of thousands of tech-savvy small nonprofits to garner the attention of online donors—a power that they did not have just a few short years ago. To maintain your online donors' loyalty, and to recruit new donors, you need to be current and forward-thinking in your online communications and fundraising. Technology moves faster than ever, and to keep up and ensure the long-term sustainability of your nonprofit, you must upgrade your Web 1.0 campaigns or risk becoming obsolete.

Nonprofit Examples of Excellence: Websites

- CURE International: cure.org

- Defenders of Wildlife: defenders.org

- National Peace Corps Association: peacecorpsconnect.org

- Stay Teen: stayteen.org

- Surfrider Foundation: surfrider.org

Nonprofit Examples of Excellence: E-newsletters

- CARE: care.org

- Conservation International: conservation.org

- Equality California: eqca.org

- Malaria No More: malarianomore.org

- Oceana: oceana.org

Nonprofit Examples of Excellence: Donate Now Campaigns

- Heal the Bay: healthebay.org

- Natural Resources Defense Council: nrdc.org

- Partners In Health: pih.org

- Save the Children: savethechildren.org

- Teachers Without Borders: teacherswithoutborders.org

Google This!

- ❑ Wikipedia static web

- ❑ Alexa top 500 global sites

- ❑ Wayback Internet time machine

- ❑ Writing for the Web

- ❑ Who uses cc?

- ❏ Purchase stock photos
- ❏ Top 10 reviews content management system software
- ❏ Wordpress for nonprofits: the complete guide
- ❏ 15 beautiful nonprofit websites wordpress
- ❏ Joomla for nonprofits
- ❏ Drupal for nonprofits
- ❏ Squarespace nonprofit examples
- ❏ Social media icons
- ❏ Top 10 reviews e-mail marketing services
- ❏ CAN-SPAM laws
- ❏ Oceana subscribe e-newsletter
- ❏ Online fundraising for nonprofit organizations linkedin group
- ❏ How to update your nonprofit report guidestar
- ❏ Giving usa 2011 executive summary
- ❏ Giving usa 2012 executive summary
- ❏ Convio benchmark report 2011
- ❏ Convio benchmark report 2012
- ❏ Blackbaud index of charitable giving
- ❏ Infographic charity and technology in the online universe
- ❏ How to launch a sustainer program
- ❏ Monthly giving
- ❏ Holiday gift programs that benefit nonprofits
- ❏ Peer-to-peer fundraising best practices
- ❏ Infographic power of social fundraising and friends asking friends

WEB 2.0
THE SOCIAL WEB

GETTING STARTED WITH SOCIAL MEDIA

Don't be afraid to fail! We've done so many things in social media that flopped. We didn't get discouraged; we learned from our mistakes and next time came back even stronger.

—*Carie Lewis, director of emerging media, Humane Society of the United States*

WEB 2.0 HAS CHANGED ONLINE COMMUNICATIONS AND FUNDRAISING FOREVER

The launch of Friendster in 2002 and then LinkedIn and Myspace in 2003 began a fundamental shift in how people and nonprofits use the Internet. The Web began to make the transition from being static to being social. In 2004 came Flickr, and then YouTube in 2005—forever changing the way we view and share photos and video. Facebook left its birthplace in higher education and opened to the masses in 2006, a defining moment that gave rise to the largest social network thus far in the Web's short history. In the same year, Twitter began to tweet. By the time Foursquare and Gowalla hit the Web and mobile devices in 2009, nonprofit communications and online fundraising campaigns were completely unrecognizable compared to what they had been just five years previously.

Today, we're all still learning and improving with each status update, tweet, and check-in. Thankfully, our mistakes are most often forgiven by our friends, followers, and fans, and our successes are increasingly rewarded with "Likes" and "Retweets." The Social Web is more casual in style and tone, and more personal in its ability to connect individuals and nonprofits with similar causes, concerns, and passions. When combined with the knowledge and power of our Web 1.0 campaigns, social media helped us finally begin to reach the full potential of the Internet for social good.

The blogosphere often touts the successes of the business sector in social media, but it was the nonprofit sector that led the way by launching Myspace Profiles and YouTube Channels in 2005, Facebook Groups in 2006, and Twitter Profiles in 2007. We are leaders in this communications revolution. Now, almost six years into using social media for social good, nonprofits collectively have the knowledge and experience to transform our sector, the Web, and philanthropy.

BEFORE YOU GET STARTED, GET ORGANIZED

The successful implementation of social media for your nonprofit requires forethought and planning. Some of the decisions you make early on will affect your social media campaigns for years. Make sure they are the right ones. Too many nonprofits have rushed in without proper training or know-how, and unfortunately have learned later on that they've made many mistakes—some of which cannot be rectified. Whether you've been using social media for years, months, or days or you have yet to get started, the information and strategies in this chapter can save you a lot of time and frustration.

1. Define Your Goals and Objectives

To lay a strong foundation for the successful long-term branding of your nonprofit on the Social Web, you need to define your primary goals and objectives. Are you using social media primarily to raise money? To secure new volunteers? To increase your website traffic? To build your online brand? To foster social good and create social change? Take an hour or two and write down five to ten goals and objectives. This will help you stay focused and give you a baseline against which you can monitor your progress.

2. Define Your Metrics and Create a Social Media ROI Spreadsheet

Once you have defined your goals and objectives, create a social media ROI spreadsheet to monitor and report your progress from month to month. In the far left column of the spreadsheet, list the metrics that you want to monitor. Next, create 12 columns for the 12 months. Finally, pick a day of the month to begin and enter the baseline metrics for the first month, then enter your progress for that month on the same day of every month thereafter. Some common metrics to monitor are website traffic, blog traffic, e-newsletter subscribers, Facebook fans, Twitter followers, online dollars raised, volunteers, and event attendees. If your nonprofit is on the right track with social media, then you'll notice an increase in the metrics from month to month over time. If not, then your social media strategy is missing something.

3. Create a Google Account and Set Up Google Alerts

The need to have a Google account will come up many times in your social media and mobile technology campaigns. Go to "google.com/ accounts > Create an account." During the sign-up process, you'll want to choose a username (such as nonprofitorgs) that matches the URLs of both your website and your social networking communities because it becomes both your profile vanity URL (google.com/ profiles/nonprofitorgs) and your Gmail account (nonprofitorgs @gmail.com).

Next, once you've set up your new Google account, sign up to receive Google Alerts via e-mail on a daily basis at google.com/alerts. Fill out a query to search "everything" for your nonprofit's name and acronym. You do not need a Google account to receive Google Alerts, but you do need one to manage them. Also, as you'll see in Chapter 5, you will need a Google account to set up a YouTube Channel properly. Google offers an incredible range of products (google.com/options) that you are likely to experiment with in coming years, so a Google account is a must for any nonprofit.

4. Be Consistent When Reserving Vanity URLs

Consistency in vanity URLs is important for print materials, e-newsletters, and e-signatures (facebook.com/nonprofitorgs, twitter.com/nonprofitorgs, youtube.com/nonprofitorgs, and so on), although if your nonprofit is just getting started with social media, then you may have some trouble reserving your first choice of vanity

URLs because there's a good chance that they have already been taken. Ideally, your social media vanity URLs should match your website URL, but if your website URL is not available on the big three (Facebook, Twitter, and YouTube), then you may need to get creative. For example, the Latin America Work Group's website is www.lawg.org, but when the organization was setting up its profiles on Facebook, Twitter, and YouTube, "lawg" was not available on all three sites. So, it went with "lawgaction" instead (facebook.com/lawgaction, twitter.com/lawgaction, and youtube.com/lawgaction).

To find out whether the URLs of your choice are available, simply enter your preferred vanity URLs in your Web browser. If you get a message that says, "That page cannot be found," that means that the URL is available. It's worth noting that in most cases you will not be able to change social media URLs at a later date, so put some serious thought into these URLs before reserving them. For organizational reasons, you could opt to use the Gmail e-mail account that you created for your nonprofit when setting up your Google account for all social media and mobile technology accounts. It will help you centralize all your efforts and reduce the amount of spam and notification e-mails sent to your work e-mail account. However, if you do opt to use your Gmail e-mail account, protect it fiercely. Go to "Gmail > Settings > Accounts and Import > Grant access to your account" and add an additional staff person (he must have a Gmail e-mail account) to prevent losing access to all your social media and mobile technology profiles and accounts in a worst-case scenario. That said, if you decide to use Gmail e-mail as your login hub, then it is best to not give interns or volunteers access.

5. Save Usernames and Passwords in a Secure Place

Create a master login sheet. Using a Word or Excel document, create a list of all the usernames, passwords, and vanity URLs for your social media and mobile technology accounts. Make sure that key staff members at your nonprofit have access to the document and that it is saved securely.

6. Use a Square Version of Your Organization's Logo as Your Avatar on Social Media Sites

It's very important that you invest the time and resources needed into designing a visually distinct, square avatar that matches the overall branding of your nonprofit. Since most nonprofit logos are horizontal, they cannot be used as your avatar on social media sites because they are automatically cropped once they are uploaded. Would you ever put a cropped logo on your website, in your e-mail newsletter, or in print materials? Of course not! Yet every day, nonprofits are sending out hundreds of thousands of tweets and status updates with completely wrecked logos. To begin branding your nonprofit on social media sites properly, start with an avatar that is a square version of your logo. After a year or so of building the brand recognition of your avatar, you can then switch and rotate square photos as avatars to spark curiosity and add variety, as long as they include a smaller version of your logo somewhere in the avatar.

7. Learn Basic HTML

Basic knowledge of Hypertext Markup Language (HTML) will make or break your social media campaigns. To add images to your blog, create custom tabs on Facebook, and/or design an e-newsletter template, you need to know basic HTML code. HTML allows you to format text and insert links and images on Web pages. Take a class or sit down for a few hours with a tutorial, just <strong> make sure that you learn <em>basic</em> HTML!</strong>

8. Experiment with Social Media Dashboards

HootSuite is a Web-based social media dashboard service that allows you to update and monitor Twitter, Facebook, Foursquare, LinkedIn, and WordPress from one dashboard. You can schedule tweets and status updates in advance (ideal for nonprofits with international audiences), easily monitor trending topics, and get access to useful statistics about your brand and its buzz on the Social Web in real time. HootSuite also offers numerous apps, making it compatible with most smartphones and tablets.

People who use social media dashboards tend to acclimate and convert for the long term. In fact, more than half of all Twitterers use a third-party dashboard tool to manage their Twitter campaigns. These tools can be incredibly useful and innovative, but make sure that you commit to not wrapping yourself in a HootSuite bubble. These tools are designed for marketers, and sometimes users can lose touch with how their individual supporters experience Twitter, Facebook, Foursquare, and other sites—which is by logging into each site individually. If you are going to use a tool like HootSuite regularly, take a break every so often. You should also never automate content using these tools, or spam each community with the same message. Every social networking community has its own unique ebb and flow, and your supporters have no interest in liking, following, or friending a robot. While these tools can help you streamline your social media campaigns, they have made poor social media managers of many. That said, other well-known social media dashboard services include TweetDeck, Threadsy, Seesmic, and CoTweet.

9. Get Buy-in from Executive Staff

For many nonprofits, getting the green light to use social media, and, more important, to invest the time and resources necessary to launch and maintain successful social media campaigns, is unfortunately still much easier said than done. This is where the age divide often becomes blatantly obvious. Many older executive staff members just don't get social media. They are deeply entrenched and often stuck in the era of Web 1.0—much to the frustration of some of their younger colleagues.

The reality is that social media is no longer new. Many nonprofits are entering their sixth or seventh year of using social media. If your nonprofit is still on the fence about social media, then it is dangerously close to becoming dysfunctional in terms of online communications and fundraising. Tell your boss that. Show her the stats. Research how other nonprofits with missions and programs similar to yours are using social media, and then let the executive staff clearly know that your nonprofit is falling behind. Be persistent. Social media is not a fad. It is a fundamental shift in how people use the Internet for social good. Failing to participate in the Social Web will be detrimental to your nonprofit in the long term.

10. Create a Simple Media Policy

An organization's social media policy should provide basic guidelines to staff members and volunteers about what is appropriate to post on social media sites, an overview of privacy and legal issues, and some general rules about using social media during office hours. The overall message should be one of empowerment, not control and restriction. Keep it simple and on the short side. Focus on the big picture and create guidelines that can be applied across many social media tools, such as

- Commit to high standards of professionalism when representing the organization online. Our goal is to build online communities in order to share our expertise and better serve our mission and programs.

- Be respectful and polite at all times—even during online disagreements.

- Delete content that is off-topic or inappropriate in character. When in doubt, get a second opinion.

- Link to online references and source material often.

- Acknowledge mistakes quickly.

- Be honest and authentic.

- Engage in conversation.

- Think before you post, and make sure that your content is accurate and factual.

- Share only content that is meant for public consumption. Don't discuss programs or campaigns that have not yet been officially launched to the public.

- Personal use of social media during breaks is allowed, but use of social media for work purposes must be approved first.

- Enjoy yourself! If you are not having fun engaging in online communities on behalf of the organization, then don't do it. Social media is not for every personality type.

11. Follow Large Organizations with a Mission and Programs Similar to Yours

Large nonprofits usually have the resources to experiment, hire consultants, and get extensive training on what works and what doesn't. Follow those whose mission and programs are similar to yours, and mimic their work. Nonprofits like Amnesty International, PETA, the American Cancer Society, the Sierra Club, and the Susan G. Komen for the Cure excel in online communications. Learn from them. Study their websites and blogs. Experience their online donation process. Subscribe to their e-newsletters. Like them on Facebook. Follow them on Twitter. Almost every action that these nonprofits take online is for a good reason. They know what works and what doesn't, they are constantly innovating and experimenting, and they are usually one or two steps ahead of most other nonprofits.

That said, have realistic expectations. Don't expect the same results from social media that the large nonprofits have. Their brands are well known and much loved. They usually have enormous e-newsletter lists and multiple communications staff members. For those reasons, large nonprofits have a huge advantage on the Social Web, but you can duplicate their success on a smaller scale.

DECIDING WHAT SOCIAL MEDIA TOOLS TO USE

How deeply your nonprofit can dive into social media is directly related to your capacity in terms of staff time. The truth is that you get out of social media what you put into it. If you can invest only 5 hours a week, then you will get the return on investment (ROI) from 5 hours of work. If you hire a social media manager who can invest 40 hours a week in engaging your supporters online, then your ROI will be significantly higher. How many social media tools your nonprofit can use effectively is directly related to the number of hours your nonprofit can invest.

If your budget is limited, you can distribute the responsibility for using various tools among different staff members, but implementing an effective social media strategy that is dispersed among multiple staff members will require strict organization and disciplined leadership. The era of "winging" it in social media is over. Your supporters and donors now expect well-executed, integrated social media campaigns.

That said, a rough estimate of the amount of time it takes on average to utilize the social media tools discussed in this book follows below. The time estimates include how long it takes to research and create content to share on the various sites, the actual time spent engaging and participating in your nonprofit's online communities, and the time necessary to monitor and report ROI. It's important to note that the time requirements for each tool are fluid and are always changing from week to week, but the estimates do provide a framework that will help you draft a realistic social media manager job description and decide what social media tools your nonprofit can utilize based on your capacity.

If your nonprofit wants to use the majority of the tools listed here effectively, then you need to hire a full-time social media manager. If you want to utilize all of them, then you need two full-time staff members. It's also worth noting that these time estimates do not include website maintenance, e-newsletter publication, Donate Now campaign management, or group texting and text-to-give campaigns, so pick and choose carefully based on what your resources allow. It's better to utilize a few tools very well than many tools poorly.

Facebook, Twitter, and YouTube: 15 Hours Weekly

As a starting point, all nonprofits should be investing time and resources in the "Big Three": Facebook, Twitter, and YouTube. Facebook is the largest social network in the world and is becoming increasingly integrated into the Social Web with every passing second. Once your nonprofit's Facebook Page has been created, it requires no more than three to five hours a week on average to maintain.

All nonprofits should also experiment with Twitter. Not everyone is a natural-born Twitterer, and it may take time to find the right person at your nonprofit to be the voice(s) behind your Twitter avatar, but it's worth the investment of resources. Though it is not as large as Facebook, Twitter is heavily used by the media, the blogosphere, and professionals from all sectors. Of the Big Three, Twitter requires the most time to utilize.

Finally, and even if your nonprofit is not yet producing videos (you can "Favorite" videos to build your channel), you should have a YouTube Channel. YouTube is the second largest search engine in the world, behind only Google. It is highly trafficked and should be the foundation for your nonprofit's video campaigns. You may later decide to expand and also use other video tools like Vimeo and Viddy, but skipping YouTube in your social media campaigns is a big mistake for the simple reason that its user base dwarfs all others. The time required to utilize YouTube will vary from week to week, but on average, you should allot five hours per week in your job description to post, create, and share video.

Flickr: 5 Hours Weekly

Uploading photos to Flickr doesn't require much time, but shooting digital photos, editing them, and then properly adding them to Flickr sets and collections with tags and titles can become time-consuming.

Nonprofits that host many events or are related to the arts, animals, nature, or international development should definitely be using Flickr. Many people today are overwhelmed by text, and photos and slideshows can often do better at communicating your message than text-heavy articles or blog posts. Flickr is the largest photo-sharing social networking community on the Web and should be your starting point for your online photo-sharing campaigns. Time and resources permitting, you can then expand to also using tools like Instagram and Facebook Photos.

LinkedIn: 5 Hours Weekly

LinkedIn is a powerhouse in ROI. Unfortunately, most nonprofits that dabbled with LinkedIn Groups in the early years did so incorrectly and abandoned their groups much too soon. Those that stuck around are beginning to reap the rewards of early adoption. Using the site for your own personal professional reasons aside, managing a LinkedIn Group and LinkedIn Company Page for your nonprofit requires a minimum time investment of five hours per week. As the site continues to grow in popularity and functionality, that amount could easily increase. At the very least, every nonprofit needs to claim its company page and then subsequently invest two to three hours per month monitoring the page.

Blogging: 10 Hours Weekly

Before 2006, blogging in the nonprofit sector had the primary purpose of giving a nonprofit a human voice—a personality or character voice that classic Web 1.0 writing does not permit. Usually the responsibility of blogging was relegated to executive or program staff, who blogged editorial opinion pieces about issues and organizational development. Today, the purpose of blogging has completely changed, and more often than not, blogging is the missing piece in a nonprofit's social media strategy.

To blog effectively, a nonprofit must allocate a minimum of 10 hours per week to blogging. That includes the time necessary to research and write material and to secure images, videos, and graphics, as well the time necessary to manage and edit guest bloggers. In the era of the Social Web, content is queen, and blogging is the easiest, most cost-effective, search engine optimization (SEO)-enhancing tool out there for publishing content. If your nonprofit takes social media seriously, so much so that you hire a social media manager, blogging should be at the top of your to-do list.

Niche Networks (Ning, Change.org, Care2, Jumo, WiserEarth, BlackPlanet): 5 to 10 Hours Weekly

There's no shortage of niche networks out there to experiment with. Ning allows nonprofits to launch their own social networking communities. Change.org and Care2 specialize in social networking focused on causes and online petitions. Jumo is an issue-based social network with a heavy emphasis on news. WiserEarth is for environmentalists. BlackPlanet, Quepasa, Bebo, Hi5, and Orkut cater to communities of color and international audiences. Over the last five years, many niche networks have come and gone, and whether these survive depends upon whether they adapt and innovate as the Web continues to evolve.

The decision to invest time in these sites depends on your supporter base. If your nonprofit primarily serves the African American community, it's worth experimenting with a group on BlackPlanet. If your nonprofit does international development in Asia or Latin America, try Hi5 or Quepasa. If your mission is one that requires privacy, such as working with victims of domestic violence, try building a closed community on Ning. There's no guarantee of return on investment, but if you have the capacity and an enthusiastic social media manager, there's no harm in dabbling to discover if one or two of these niche networks are a fit for your nonprofit.

Peer-to-Peer Fundraising Networks (Razoo, Crowdrise, FirstGiving, GlobalGiving): 5 to 10 Hours Weekly

It's a brave new world in online fundraising. Letting go of control and empowering others to raise funds for your organization by creating fundraising pages on peer-to-peer fundraising networks can either result in hundreds of new online donors or be a colossal flop. Your success depends on your mission and how engaged and passionate your supporters are for your cause. If your nonprofit regularly hosts events that require people to solicit donations from friends and family, like marathons and walk-a-thons, peer-to-peer fundraising is an absolute must. It can also work well for nonprofits that respond to natural disasters or crises. In addition, peer-to-peer fundraising campaigns can produce positive results when they are offered for birthday, holiday, graduation, or memorial gifts. If your nonprofit meets these requirements, pick one site and invest 5 to 10 hours a week encouraging your fundraisers, thanking them, and providing tips and training.

Location-Based Communities (Facebook Places, Foursquare, Gowalla): 5 to 10 Hours Weekly

Location-based communities have a big role to play in the future of nonprofit communications. As with Facebook in 2007 and Twitter in 2008, the early adopters began experimenting with location-based communities in 2009. This is a trend that will evolve dramatically over the next few years and is likely to spur hundreds of new Web tools to experiment with and be overwhelmed by, but the best social media managers will adapt quickly. Much of the work involved with these tools will take place on smartphones and tablets and, depending on your check-in volume, will require 5 to 10 hours a week.

What about Myspace?

In its heyday in 2006 and 2007, Myspace was an incredibly vibrant community of artists, musicians, and impassioned activists and do-gooders. Nonprofits like Invisible Children and To Write Love on Her Arms were born from Myspace. At a time when Facebook was primarily used by college-educated individuals from the middle and upper classes, Myspace was open, diverse, creative, and seemingly the epitome of an online grassroots community.

Then late in 2007 and throughout 2008, the spam on Myspace started to become overwhelming, while at the same time the naysayers and fearmongers were growing larger and louder. The mainstream media and higher education essentially flipped out over the "dangers of social networking," and Myspace took the brunt of it. The birth of social networking on a mass scale was messy and chaotic, and at times fear and paranoia ran amok. As a result, by late 2008, most of the middle-class white Americans who had initially feared Myspace and social networking began to flock to the clean, neat Facebook community. The dangers of social networking quickly evolved into "opportunities," and the blogosphere lit up with rants against Myspace, the newly dubbed "ghetto" of the Web, and sang the praises of Facebook and Internet superstar Mark Zuckerberg.

The rise and fall (and perhaps rise again) of Myspace taught nonprofit communicators that were paying attention some very important lessons that we should learn from and never forget. First, class and race issues play out in social media just as they do in real life. Much of the media and blog coverage of Myspace was elitist and at its worst, racist and classist and offensive to many Myspace users (at the time, there were more than 200,000,000 of them worldwide). As a whole, the nonprofit sector, caught up in its own Facebook euphoria, failed miserably at being a voice for tolerance and civility in the Myspace vs. Facebook war propagated by tech blogs and the media. Sadly, many nonprofits abandoned their communities on Myspace much too soon.

Second, the time that nonprofits invested in building their Myspace communities was time well spent. When the early adopters of Myspace (see Acknowledgments) made the transition to Facebook and Twitter, their Myspace communities made the transition with them. Social networking communities are migrant communities. They will move with you from one community to the next if you make a concerted effort to ask them to do so. That said, it's no coincidence that some of the most popular nonprofits on Facebook and Twitter today were the pioneers of social networking for social good on Myspace.

Finally, the rise and fall of Myspace teaches us that nothing is certain on the Social Web. In 2006 and 2007, Myspacers would never have believed that the site would fall so far and so fast. There's always a Next Big Thing. Friends, followers, and fans can be fickle. Embrace Facebook, Twitter, and YouTube, but don't assume that they will be around 5 or 10 years from now. In the Myspace vs. Facebook war, there's no doubt that the smarter and more innovative site won, but when the Next Big Thing comes along, let's commit to making it a more respectful, civil transition.

All that said, does your nonprofit need to be on Myspace? Without a crystal ball, that is a very tough call to make. Tens of thousands of individuals are still active on the site daily, but Myspace's numbers have shrunk dramatically. It's hard to come back after that. If your nonprofit had a Myspace community but has abandoned it in recent years, then at the very least you should log back in, sync your Myspace community with your Twitter feed, and continue to log in on a monthly basis to approve new friends. If your nonprofit has never used Myspace and you come from the Facebook and Twitter world, then Myspace will most likely be unappealing or feel cumbersome to you. It's a complicated site that requires HTML knowledge. Begin to use it now only if your supporters have indicated clearly that you need to have a presence there.

ELEVEN QUALITIES OF AN EFFECTIVE SOCIAL MEDIA MANAGER

Despite all the buzz about social media, the reality is that your social media campaigns are only as good as the human being(s) behind them. Going "viral" on social media sites is extremely rare, and instantaneous success is a myth. Being an effective social media manager is both an art and a skill. Some personalities are more inclined to be successful at managing and inspiring online communities, but the vast majority of practitioners will need months, if not years, to learn to produce social media success through a process of trial and error. For your nonprofit to succeed on social media sites, make sure that your social media manager (a.k.a. new media manager, digital marketing manager, or some similar title) has most of the following qualities.

1. Has a Passion for His Cause and for Social Media

You can hear it in his voice and read it in his tweets. A good social media manager has passion for his cause(s) and enjoys participating in social media. The best social media practitioners will express their personality with a dash of attitude and a bit of flair, and will be comfortable articulating their opinions online. They don't need to be brash or controversial in their opinions, but they do not shy away from asserting their viewpoints on behalf of your nonprofit, its mission, and its programs. They have an instinctive ability to balance confidence in their opinions with humility. Arrogance and inflated egos are a huge turn-off in the social media for social good arena. Passion and enthusiasm are not. The best social media managers understand the difference.

2. Is Friendly, Patient, and Responsive

Effective social media managers enjoy engaging with and responding to comments on social media sites. They relish discussing ideas and issues online, and they do it with patience and kindness. They are attentive to their communities on an almost daily basis. They express gratitude for support, and they acknowledge questions and concerns. They have the unique ability to defuse troublesome (and sometimes obnoxious and rude) personalities with kind, but firm commentary. It's a real skill to navigate and guide the online commons, and to know how and when to react.

That said, a good social media manager also knows the difference between expressing gratitude effectively and over-the-top schmoozing. Authenticity, or the lack thereof, will make or break your nonprofit's social media campaigns. Individuals with friendly personalities who have strength of character and moral conviction make the best social media managers. Don't underestimate the importance of this position at your organization. Your social media manager's online voice represents who you are, what you do, and what your nonprofit stands for.

3. Is Creative and Detail-Oriented

Creativity is what makes exceptional social media campaigns stand out from the rest. Doing something different with a set of tools that tens of thousands of other nonprofits are using is the trademark of an exceptional social media manager. Her brain is constantly at work dreaming up new campaigns, and rather than shying away from being different and taking risks, she embraces it. Social media manager is not a tech position. It's a communications and development position where good writing skills are of paramount importance. When hiring or training for this position, hone in on the person's creative experience, not her tech experience.

Also, the ability to manage and jump between numerous online communities requires the ability to multitask. Social media managers are often present and engaging online in five or more communities on any given day, and often simultaneously. To do so effectively, they need to be detail-oriented and organized. Someone who is easily overwhelmed will struggle with social media. Creativity combined with being detail-oriented is the winning combination of skills for an effective social media manager.

4. Has Experience in Online Communications

Just because someone is 19 and came of age using Facebook in his personal life does not mean that he can manage and implement your online communities on social media sites successfully. Untrained interns were fine two or three years ago, when the Social Web was still in its infancy and everyone was experimenting, but that era is over. If your budget is limited and you can afford only interns or volunteers, make sure they get some training before they become the voice of your nonprofit. There are plenty of low-cost Webinars out there that can provide your interns with a basic foundation in Web 1.0 commu-nication, fundraising, and social media how-to.

The truth is, in terms of results in social media, you get what you pay for, and if you want the best person for the job, you will need someone who has at least a year or two of professional experience in Web 1.0. He will have written content for the Web, published an e-newsletter, blogged, and experimented with various online fundraising campaigns. It's rare that someone with no background in online communications or fundraising instinctively understands how to use social media to build an online brand.

5. Reads Blogs about Social Media and Mobile Technology

A good social media manager will be a regular reader of *Mashable*, *TechCrunch*, *Social Media Today*, *Social Times*, *Mobile Marketing Watch*, *All Facebook*, *About Foursquare*, *Nonprofit Tech 2.0*, *Beth's Blog*, *TechSoup*, *NTEN*, and other such blogs. Social media moves very quickly, and your nonprofit will fall behind or miss opportunities to explore the Next Big Thing if your social media manager is not regu-larly browsing these blogs for breaking news about tools, upgrades, and emerging trends. Seriously. Reading these blogs on a regular basis needs to be a line item in every social media manager's job description. That said, social bookmarking sites like Digg, Delicious, Reddit, and StumbleUpon can be useful for discovering and organiz-ing blog and news content related to the use of social media and mobile technology in the nonprofit sector.

6. Is an Early Adopter

The nonprofits that are the most successful in social media today were on Myspace and YouTube in 2005 and 2006. They have time on their side. Online communities grow in number over time, exponentially. The earlier you start, the more likely you are to be successful. Not only that, but online communities also tend to grow the fastest during the early adoption phase. They're not interesting or buzz-worthy once tens of thousands of other nonprofits are using them. In fact, in the era of the Social Web, and even more so on the Mobile Web, early adoption in and of itself is a strategy. Those who do it first tend to do it best.

Again, some of the best-known early adopters in the nonprofit space were the Humane Society of the United States, Oxfam International, the National Wildlife Federation, PETA, and the Save Darfur Coalition. They are great nonprofits to watch and mimic because being an early adopter is now seemingly part of their overall online strategy. They've learned over the years that the initial investment of time necessary for early adoption usually pays off down the road.

7. Is Not Overly Confident about Her Social Media Skills

Overconfidence about their social media skills prevents most social media managers from getting the necessary training. Every second of every day, nonprofits on Facebook, Twitter, YouTube, Flickr, WordPress, Foursquare, and other social media are making obvious mistakes that are counterproductive to their presence on these sites. Please get training! Take Webinars, attend boot camps, or go to conferences that focus on the how-to of social media. The most valuable advice should be practical and should come from someone who actually manages online communities and works with these tools every single day. Be skeptical of the self-proclaimed social media mavens, rock stars, or experts who have no practical experience running, maintaining, and building online communities around causes or nonprofit brands on social networking sites.

8. Thinks like a Journalist

Well-written, timely content is what drives the Social Web. Old news is not share-, like-, or retweet-worthy. Increasingly, nonprofit communicators and social media practitioners need to consider themselves to be reporters for their cause and nonprofit—always listening, responding rapidly, and sometimes even "Live! On location!" This is why blogging has become so central to a successful social media strategy. It allows social media managers to respond to breaking news by quickly and easily creating content that can be posted and hopefully shared by others on the Social Web.

Thinking like a journalist also means reporting regularly on events and campaigns as they unfold, and sharing those news stories with your online communities. In this case, your social media manager definitely needs a passion for the cause and for writing. In the coming years, thinking and acting like a journalist will become even more important with the rise of Internet TV. Your social media manager(s) will be playing not only the role of a print journalist for your nonprofit, but also the role of a broadcast journalist, streaming live "On location!" Ready or not, TV is about to get a lot more social—and you can bet that the early adopters in the nonprofit sector are already preparing, researching, and implementing "TV" campaigns.

9. Is Mobile

Social media managers should be comfortable with the idea of posting status updates and tweets from any location at any time, when necessary. Whether we like it or not, the news cycle is now 24/7, and as a journalist for your cause, you need to be, too. Mobile technology enables that. Increasingly laptops are becoming cumbersome in comparison to smartphones and tablets, and as the Mobile Web continues to expand, so will the tools that have been uniquely designed for smartphones and tablets. The best social media and mobile technology practitioners will embrace these new tools, experiment with them, and be willing to sacrifice some of their free time outside of traditional office hours in order to be available to their communities 24/7.

10. Is Willing to Mesh His Personal Life
with His Professional Life Online

It's a whole new Web. It's social. It's mobile. It's public. You have to be willing to be on Facebook personally or LinkedIn professionally.

You have to be willing to merge some of your personal life with your professional life online. This is where age really comes into play in terms of social media adoption. To the younger folks, not being on Facebook or LinkedIn just seems silly. It's akin to a story of walking five miles to school in the snow with holes in your shoes. The concept seems ancient.

For a good social media manager, privacy is a concern, but it is not a crippling one. She takes responsibility for her own privacy and takes steps to protect it where and when she wants to. She is educated about privacy settings on various social networking sites. She doesn't post anything she doesn't want her boss or her parents to see, but beyond that, mixing her personal and professional lives online is something that she is willing to do in order to be the best advocate she can be for her cause and her nonprofit. If you don't want to be on Facebook or LinkedIn, then don't. It's not for everyone, but you need to understand that the line between the personal and the professional is becoming increasingly blurred and meshed together. If you want a future career in online communications and fundraising, there are basic levels of privacy, like complete anonymity, that you will have to sacrifice.

11. Takes Steps to Prevent Social Media Burnout

For all the social good it can do, social media does have a downside. Nonprofit practitioners are bombarded with messages all day long on Facebook, Twitter, YouTube, Foursquare, and so on. It can be too much for the brain to process sometimes, especially since much of the content coming out of the nonprofit communities is related to sad, depressing news (war, rape, overpopulation, poverty, depletion of environmental resources, animal cruelty and wildlife extinction, and so on). A good social media manager knows when to draw the line and takes time away from her communities when necessary. Here are some tips to avoid social media burnout:

- *Pick a time to shut it all down at the end of the day, and stick to it.* Occasionally you will need to work during the evening hours, but most of the time you will not. At some point in the early evening, your Web usage should switch from professional to personal.

- *Do not work more than 10 minutes on the weekends.* One status update or tweet per weekend is enough. During special events or campaigns, you will sometimes need to put in more time, but in general the Web goes into sleep mode professionally on the weekends. That said, many Web users use social media for personal reasons on the weekends, and posting a status update or tweet on the weekends can really stand out, since most other nonprofits are completely offline.

- *Pick one social networking community that you will keep personal so that you can also enjoy social networking for fun.* If all your social networking is for work and none is for fun, you will burn out.

- *Sometimes leave the smartphone at home.* Increasingly, this is becoming more of a challenge with the rise of mobile social networking and location-based communities, but a dinner out or shopping with friends without checking in or tweeting is rejuvenating.

- *Don't take your smartphone and/or tablet with you on vacation.* Seriously! There are Internet cafés worldwide if you need to connect with friends while you're away.

- *Take time for lunch. Get out of the office and away from the computer, and put your smartphone away.* Say hi to people on the streets. Open doors and smile. Make human, face-to-face connections, too.

- *Breathe deeply, exercise, and treat yourself.* Managing social media is a mentally and physically demanding job. Often people are intensely engaged and frozen in their posture for hours at a time, holding their breath, and being indoors all day long. Commit to doing breathing exercises, joining a gym, going for regular walks, and having an occasional massage or mani/pedi. You have to get away from social media from time to time. You have to.

- *Connect with friends and family in person and on the phone, too.* Social networking and texting are the most popular ways to stay in touch these days, but if you're not careful and lose your balance, then you can become isolated and lonely in your relationships as well. Calling and in-person visits need to be a priority. Most social media managers will be surrounded by staff members and connecting with others all day long, but for those who work from home, this advice is especially for you.

- *Don't waste your time or energy with mean, grumpy, disrespectful people.* The longer you manage online communities, the more the line between respectful disagreement and rude, egotistical ranting will become blatantly obvious. Mean, grumpy, disrespectful people are a waste of your precious time and energy. Nothing you say will sway their tone or end their ranting. Let them exercise their First Amendment rights elsewhere, because these miserable, angry, ranting people will only bring you and your community down. Delete, block, and move on without a second thought. In general, these types of online personalities are not active in nonprofit communities. Most social media managers will have to deal with them only a couple of times a year unless they work for a nonprofit that deals with controversial issues, such as abortion, immigration, politics, or religion. In that case, it's more likely to be a daily experience. For those of you in that situation, you need to take extra effort to prevent burnout, and hopefully you are getting the support you need from the executive staff at your organization.

FINAL WORDS:
DIVERSIFY YOUR BRAND ONLINE

Social media has transformed the Web, and most social media practitioners would say for the better, but it does have long-term implications for privacy and for the Internet as a whole. Nonprofits have an important role to play in discussions of these issues as advocates for social good on the Web. Make a commitment to educate yourself on topics such as privacy, fair use, transparency, intellectual property, censorship, corporate control, and net neutrality—not just in relation to social media, but with regard to all emerging technologies. The Electronic Frontier Foundation (eff.org), the Berkman Center for Internet and Society (cyber.law.harvard.edu), and the Save the Internet Coalition (savetheinternet.com) are nonprofits that are committed solely to those issues. Pardon the soapbox, but as a nonprofit social media practitioner, it is your civic duty to be aware and to take action when necessary.

That said, nonprofits would also be wise to ponder the interdependent relationship that they now have with for-profit social media companies. It's unprecedented, and except for the common complaint of the lack of customer service, the relationship thus far has been mutually beneficial. However, some of these companies may not be around in 10 years. It's very important that your nonprofit think long-term and diversify its brand across many platforms and communication channels, such as Facebook, Twitter, YouTube, Flickr, Foursquare, blogging, e-newsletters, group text messaging, and others. One thing is absolutely certain in social media, and that is that it is constantly in a state of flux.

Google This!

- ❏ Wikipedia social web
- ❏ Diosa social media webinars
- ❏ Skloog history of social media
- ❏ Social media statistics
- ❏ Wikipedia url
- ❏ Wikipedia html
- ❏ Html tutorial
- ❏ Html tutorial youtube
- ❏ 4096 color wheel
- ❏ Wikipedia list of social networking websites
- ❏ Youtube did you know 2.0 and 3.0
- ❏ 10 social media metrics nonprofit download roi spreadsheet
- ❏ Social media for nonprofit organizations linkedin group
- ❏ Google products for nonprofit organizations linkedin group
- ❏ Google.com/nonprofits
- ❏ Social media policy nonprofit
- ❏ Environmental defense fund social media guidelines
- ❏ Social media manager job description nonprofit
- ❏ Race class social media myspace

FACEBOOK AND FACEBOOK APPS

Facebook has been a highly effective tool in communicating the message of the Pancreatic Cancer Action Network, but it also allows our fans to support one another. Many openly share advice about grief and caring for a loved one living with pancreatic cancer. That's what makes Facebook, and social media in general, so powerful. It provides the ability for people and nonprofits to connect with one another in a way that is open and meaningful."

—Allison Nassour, social media manager,
Pancreatic Cancer Action Network

THE BIG PICTURE:
SOCIAL NETWORKING

By the time this book hits bookstores and e-readers worldwide, the Facebook community will probably be well over 750 million people. Facebook is the Social Network (pun intended). As a website, its primary strength has always been its clean, simple, orderly interface, with only mildly intrusive advertising. It was launched with the primary goal of connecting people to one another—new friends, old friends, family members, and work colleagues. Its founders have remained committed to that primary goal and design aesthetic since its founding in 2004, which in turn has made it the largest online social network in the world.

Every day hundreds of millions of people throughout the globe are connecting with one another and sharing photos, videos, news, and personal information with the Facebook community. For the majority of Millennials (also known as Gen Y), social networking is a daily routine. They have little or no discomfort or hesitation in sharing stories and images of their daily lives through "Status Updates" to their Facebook "Friends," and despite the conventional wisdom, they're much smarter about the privacy and safety aspects of social networking than the older folks give them credit for.

Most of Gen X "gets" social networking. The members of this generation came of age at the height of Web 1.0, and the transition to the Social Web has been an easy, almost natural progression. That's not so true of the baby boomers. Initially, most boomers were very resistant to social networking. Boomers who were in positions of leadership at nonprofits, and their resistance to and fears of social networking, were a source of intense frustration for many younger nonprofit professionals during those years of early adoption. Today, though, most boomers have come around. Facebook is getting wrinkles, as they say.

All that said, Facebook has now reached critical mass in the United States, and the number of users globally is soaring. Over the last few years, it has become deeply entrenched in the online lives of people of all ages, races, and economic and political backgrounds. Almost every nonprofit can now argue that it needs to have a presence on Facebook because that's "where our supporters are." To take that a step further, increasingly, if your nonprofit does not have a presence on Facebook, then it does not exist to hundreds of millions of people worldwide, and it's through Facebook Pages that nonprofits can best tap into the power of Facebook and make themselves available to the Facebook masses.

INTRODUCTION TO FACEBOOK PAGES

All websites need a revenue model in order to be sustainable, and rather than charging its members to use the site, Facebook launched Facebook Pages in November of 2006 to lay the foundation for its wildly profitable Facebook Ads program. The decision to allow brands to create Facebook Pages and publish content to the news feeds lured in millions of businesses, nonprofits, and universities that over the years have purchased billons of dollars of advertising; sent trillions of e-mails, tweets, and text messages asking customers and supporters to "Like Us on Facebook!"; and helped Facebook become the social networking powerhouse that it is today. The relationship between Facebook and the brands that utilize Facebook Pages is a symbiotic one from which both benefit.

If your nonprofit has not yet created a Facebook Page, then while you are logged into your personal account, go to facebook.com/pages and select "Create Page." From there, select "Company, Organization, or Institution," and then select your category of "Nonprofit Organization" or "Non-Governmental Organization (NGO)" from the pop-down menu. For your Facebook Page name, spell out the complete name of your nonprofit to best optimize search engine results. You cannot change the name of your Facebook Page later, so make sure that you do it right the first time. Also, do not create a "Cause or Topic" page for your nonprofit's primary Facebook Page. Those function differently (and a bit mysteriously) and are better for campaigns like "Save the Whales" or "Support a Green Economy."

That said, if you do not want to be on Facebook personally, then you can also go to facebook.com/pages, select "Create Page," and follow the instructions above, except when prompted, select the "I do not have a Facebook account" option and complete the page creation process. In the past, many nonprofits were unaware that you could create a Facebook Page without a personal profile and consequently converted a personal profile into a profile for a brand—for example, first name "Amnesty" and last name "International." Doing so is in violation of Facebook's Terms of Service and runs the risk of your profile's being deleted. Many nonprofits have also turned personal profiles into brand profiles simply because they did not know how to set up a presence for their nonprofit properly on Facebook. If you are one of them, Facebook launched an appeal process to convert a profile to a page in April 2011. To begin the process, go to the Facebook Help Center (facebook.com/help) and search "converting your profile into a page" to locate the "business page migration appeal form."

Once you have created your Facebook Page, uploaded your square avatar, and filled out the basic information required, then you're ready to start posting status updates and asking people to like your page. When you have 25 likes, you can reserve a vanity URL for your Facebook Page, such as facebook.com/nonprofitorgs, by visiting facebook.com/username, so try to reach that number as quickly as possible by asking staff members, volunteers, and friends to like your new Facebook Page.

ELEVEN FACEBOOK PAGES
BEST PRACTICES FOR NONPROFITS

One of the biggest mistakes that nonprofits have made in their social media campaigns is to assume that because someone uses Facebook regularly in her personal life, she must also know how to use

Facebook professionally. It's one thing to chat with friends and family on Facebook, and quite another to build and promote a nonprofit brand successfully inside the Facebook community. Facebook is the second most visited website in the world and is reshaping the Internet as we know it with every passing day, yet many nonprofits still relegate their Facebook Page to volunteers and interns who have no background in online communications or fundraising. However well-intentioned these people may be, that has led to some poorly executed Facebook campaigns. More than ever with the launch of Facebook Community Pages and Facebook Places Pages, clearly understanding the Facebook tool set and etiquette is paramount for your nonprofit's success on Facebook.

1. Find Your Facebook Voice

Ninety percent of the power of a Facebook Page is in the status updates. Most fans don't hang out on your Facebook Page, browsing through photos, videos, and past posts on your wall. Rather, 90 percent of their experience with your Facebook Page will occur through status updates in their news feed(s). As the admin of your nonprofit's page, your number one priority should be to find out what kind of content from your nonprofit your fans want to read and engage with. You'll know through receiving comments and thumbs ups on your status updates, or the lack thereof, whether you are finding your Facebook voice. It may take a few months of trial and error, but just start experimenting. Test different tones of voice. Add some personality. Share links to your Flickr slideshows or YouTube videos. Post inspirational quotes and powerful statistics. Post comments in response to comments and thumbs ups. You can also ask questions using Facebook Questions (facebook.com/questions). When your Facebook community is engaged and active, then you've succeeded in finding your Facebook voice; however, this is much easier said than done, so keep experimenting.

2. Always Share a Link, Photo, or Video in Status Updates

Never waste an opportunity to drive traffic from Facebook to your website, blog, YouTube Channel, or somewhere else. Always share a link, photo, or video in a status update. It makes your status updates richer and more visibly appealing because it will attach thumbnails of images to them, and thus you're much more likely to earn comments and thumbs ups. That said, if you share only your own content, you'll cross that thin line between community building and overmarketing. Mix it up! Share breaking news related to your organization's mission, trending posts from the blogosphere, popular videos from YouTube, or striking photos from Flickr. Most important, make sure that the link, photo, or video does indeed attach a thumbnail to your status update. Otherwise, people will tend to ignore it.

3. Post No More than One or Two Status Updates per Day (or Less!)

Large national and international nonprofits with well-known and much-loved brands have a different experience on Facebook from that of most small to medium-size nonprofits. They usually have lots of fresh content to share, and their fans are much less likely to "Unlike" their page if they overshare on Facebook. Small to medium-size nonprofits, however, should err on the side of caution. Less is so much more. The law of diminishing returns starts to kick in if you post multiple status updates every day. People start to tune you out, or, even worse, they "Hide" you from their news feed or unlike your page altogether. One status update per day is fine, but four to six per week is better. If you absolutely must post two per day, then post one in the morning and the other in the afternoon. That said, it's also worth noting that an occasional status update posted in the evening or on a Saturday or Sunday tends to produce high levels of engagement.

4. Do Not Automate Content and Sync Facebook with Other Social Networking Sites

There are plenty of tools available that will allow you to post the same content to multiple social networking communities with one click, but don't be tempted by them. As discussed in Chapter 2, it's very important for you to understand that each online community is unique, with its own ebb and flow of content. Five or six tweets a day is completely acceptable on Twitter, but posting that number of status updates on Facebook is an absolute worst practice. It's better to work one community correctly than to do many poorly. Authentically posting four to six status updates a week on Facebook and a couple of tweets a day on Twitter isn't that time-consuming. Your Facebook community wants to know that there is a real human being behind those status updates, not a bot. Remember, community building comes first and marketing second. Every single status update that you send out should be the result of a couple of minutes of thought, preparation, and personality.

5. Send "Updates" at Least Once or Twice a Month

Admins can send group messages known as updates to those who like their page by going to "Edit Page > Marketing > Send an Update." These updates then arrive in your fans' "Messages > Other." That said, most fans will not read your updates; however, enough will to make it worth the time to send them out once or twice a month. Keep them brief, and always attach a link. In terms of content, engage your fans in updates with success stories, urgent calls to action, and the occasional fundraising pitch.

6. Encourage Staff Members and Volunteers to Be Active on Your Page

The truth is that it's tough for many admins to find their Facebook voice. Even some of the best nonprofit communicators sometimes struggle to earn comments and thumbs ups on their status updates, but it's crucial to keep trying because only status updates with activity get exposure in the "Top News" news feed (the default news feed that users see when they log in to Facebook). No one besides Facebook knows exactly how the "Recent News" algorithm works, but it is certain that not all status updates show up in the news feeds, and the less exposure your nonprofit gets in the news feed(s), the less powerful your Facebook Page.

To help maximize the exposure of your status updates and their news feed potential, definitely encourage staff members and volunteers to post comments and give thumbs ups regularly. A reasonable goal to begin with is to earn at least one comment and three thumbs ups on each status update for every 1,000 fans. Hopefully, you can double those numbers within three months. The activity by staff members and volunteers is also likely to spark additional comments and thumbs ups from your fans, thus increasing your news feed(s) exposure. Not only that, but the more comments your nonprofit receives, the faster your page will grow in fans because comments also show up in users' activity streams.

7. Have More than One Administrator for Your Page

It's wise to prepare for the worst-case scenario. Sometimes staff members or volunteers will leave your nonprofit abruptly without notice. To prevent them from taking your Facebook Page with them, make sure that your nonprofit's Facebook Page has at least two admins. To add an admin to your page, you must first become a Facebook friend of the new admin, then go to "Edit Page > Manage Admins" to search for and add admin rights. After you have added a new admin, don't feel bad if you "Unfriend" her—especially if the new admin is your boss. There is nothing improper in terms of etiquette in wanting to separate your personal and professional lives on Facebook. People need to respect that decision.

8. Use the "Favorites" Functionality

If your nonprofit is national or international and has many chapters, then favorite the Facebook Pages of your chapters on your nonprofit's primary Facebook Page so that it can serve as a hub for your nonprofit's presence on Facebook. Do your funders have Facebook Pages? Favorite them too. Do you have a celebrity spokesperson? Favorite her page as well. Do you work in partnership with other nonprofits? Add them to your favorites. The trick is to let them know that you have added them to your favorites by either posting on their wall or tagging them in a status update. Using the favorites functionality is a subtle form of partnership building and appreciation. Odds are that they will return the favor and add you to their favorites (or mention you in a status update, a tweet, or somewhere else). It's a phenomenon that is unique to social media. The more generous you are in sharing some of your social media spotlight with others, the more it eventually comes back to shine on your nonprofit. To add a page to your favorites, simply go to the page you want to favorite and on the left side select "Add to My Page's Favorites."

9. "Tag" Other Pages to Build Partnerships

Facebook's tagging functionality enables admins to post status updates on other Facebook Pages' walls. The first impulse of many admins is to tag in order to self-promote their nonprofit's page on other organizations' walls, but in reality tagging better serves the page that is being tagged because the tagger is broadcasting to its fans the page being tagged. The tagging functionality is most beneficial in terms of increasing your nonprofit's generosity score. Like promoting other pages in your favorites, promoting other pages via tagging also reflects well upon your nonprofit and helps build partnerships within the Facebook community. Again, this is a phenomenon that is unique to social media. The more you selflessly and generously promote others, the more it eventually comes back to benefit your nonprofit.

To tag another page, such as that of a funder or a partner, admins must first like the page. Then, when writing a status update on your own page, type "@" and the first few letters of the page you want to tag. The page will then appear in a pop-down menu. Select it, and the page name will appear in your status update as a link. Finish writing your status update and then share. The result is that in addition to your status update being posted on your own wall and in the news feed(s) of your fans, it is also posted on the wall of the page that was tagged. If the admin of the page that was tagged is paying attention to his community, he will notice your generous gesture and hopefully return the favor.

That said, tagging shouldn't be approached with the objective of receiving something in return. Tag other pages only as a genuine expression of generosity or to share information that is relevant to your mission; otherwise, your fans will think that you are tag spamming. The idea of promoting others to your fans is a hard concept for many traditional nonprofit communicators to wrap their heads around, but once you've been managing communities on social networking sites for six months or more, you'll begin to notice an obvious correlation between promoting others and reciprocity.

10. Integrate Your Facebook Page into Your Website, E-newsletter, Blog, Print Materials, and "Thank You" Landing Pages and E-mails

Many nonprofits struggle with increasing their fan base on Facebook. Truth be told, there's a lot of Facebook hype in the blogosphere that seeds the idea that if you build it, they will come. In most cases, that's just not true, especially for small and medium-size nonprofits. You need to heavily promote your Facebook Page and integrate it into your website, your e-newsletters, your blog, and your print materials for your fan base to grow. During the initial launch of your Facebook Page, you will need to give your Facebook community a jump start by announcing your page in your e-newsletter. Those nonprofits that do not have an e-newsletter are definitely at a disadvantage because most new fans do come from e-newsletters. After that, to sustain a steady growth of your fan base, you will need to integrate your Facebook Page into your Web and print promotional materials by adding

- A Facebook icon on your website's home page and blog.

- A Facebook icon inside every edition of your e-newsletter.

- A Facebook link in your e-mail signature. It helps tremendously if you can implement this organization-wide.

- A Facebook pitch in print promotional materials, such as postcards, fundraising appeals, newsletters, and annual reports.

- A Facebook pitch on your "Thanks for Your Donation!" landing page and e-mails.

Except for large, very well-known brands, going viral on Facebook is mostly a myth. You have to promote your page to build your fan base.

11. Integrate your Facebook Page into Your Mobile Campaigns

Facebook has a full-featured mobile website at m.facebook.com. If your nonprofit has a mobile website or a smartphone app, make sure to link to the mobile version of your Facebook Page (such as, m.facebook.com/wildaid) on your mobile website and in your smartphone app(s); otherwise, your status updates will be very difficult to read on mobile browsers. The same is true of group text messages. If you ask your text subscribers to like your page in text messages, definitely link to the mobile version of your Facebook Page.

FIVE ADVANCED FACEBOOK BEST PRACTICES FOR NONPROFITS

Once your nonprofit has found its Facebook voice and mastered the basic functionality of Facebook Pages, then you're ready to take your campaigns to the next level. That said, as you experiment and go deeper into the Facebook Page tool set, never lose sight of the fact that 90 percent of the power of a Facebook Page is in the status updates. The other 10 percent is found in the advanced best practices listed here.

1. Create Custom Tabs

Using the Facebook App Platform or a third-party iframe tab app, you can create custom tabs as long as you know basic HTML. You can add images and graphics that prompt users to subscribe to your e-newsletter, make a donation, take action, or follow you on Twitter, Foursquare, or another community. You can also embed videos using the <embed> code directly from your YouTube Channel. Additionally, you can set a custom tab as your default landing tab by going to "Edit Page > Manage Permissions > Default Landing Tab." If you do so, when potential new fans visit your Facebook Page, instead of seeing your wall, they will see the tab that you chose as your default landing tab. For examples of custom tabs and custom default landing tabs, see the Facebook Pages of the Not for Sale Campaign (facebook.com/ notforsalecampaign), the Lupus Foundation of America (facebook .com/lupusfoundationofamerica), and SOS Children's Villages (facebook.com/soschildrensvillages).

2. Utilize Apps

There are a handful of Facebook "Apps" that can be useful to your nonprofit. The Causes app (causes.com) allows you to build a community of activists, donors, and fundraisers for your nonprofit's cause inside of Facebook. This app is worth exploring, but have realistic expectations. Most nonprofits have not been successful in using Causes for fundraising, but it is constantly evolving and improving. As online donors continue to grow in number and embrace new fundraising platforms, an investment of time in building your Causes community could pay off at a later date. The Humane Society of the United States has been very successful in utilizing Causes, and it often features its Causes tab on its Facebook Page (facebook.com/humanesociety).

Involver.com offers a suite of apps that allow you to create Twitter, YouTube, Flickr, RSS, or custom tabs, and anyone can use up to two for free. Also, in Facebook's App Directory (facebook.com/apps), you will discover a wide variety of polling apps and numerous content-sharing apps. It doesn't hurt to explore and test apps, but it's important that you stay focused on the fact that most of the power of Facebook is in the status updates. Don't get distracted by all the shiny apps! Also, any kind of app that fans have to "Add" to use or view (with the exception of Causes) should be avoided. People can become easily annoyed by invitations or prompts to add apps.

3. Add "Share" and/or "Like" Functionality to Your Website and Blog

Adding the ability for people to easily share your content directly from your website or blog is worth the time, effort, and expense. There are millions of people who want to help propagate social good on the Web by simply sharing your nonprofit's message with their friends and family through Facebook, Twitter, LinkdIn, or e-mail. You just need to make it easy for them to do so. Depending on what content management system (CMS) and blog platform you use, you will probably have to add a plug-in or use a service like ShareThis (sharethis.com) or AddThis (addthis.com). Technically, this functionality may be a challenge to set up initially, but it can radically transform your traffic and exposure on the Social Web. A nonprofit called Greater Than AIDS is a great example of a nonprofit that has successfully integrated share functionality into its website (greaterthanaids.org).

Also, Facebook offers a widget as part of its Open Social Graph initiative that allows you to put "Like" buttons on pages inside of your website and your blog. These are not to be confused with the Facebook Like Boxes (found under "Edit Page > Marketing > Add a Like Box to Your Website") that enable people to like your Facebook Page directly from your website or blog. Rather, the "Like" buttons can be placed on every page of your website, and when people click to like the content of the Web page, a link is then added to their Facebook activity stream on their wall that links directly back to your website or blog. For example, visit the website for People for the Ethical Treatment of Animals at peta.org. It has integrated "Like" buttons throughout its website. If you were to click a "Like" button on a PETA page entitled "Help Abused Circus Elephants," then a link entitled "Help Abused Circus Elephants" would be posted on your personal wall on Facebook that would link back to the PETA page. Many friends and family of Facebook users like to browse walls, thus increasing the likelihood of increased traffic to your website. The buttons themselves are a simple piece of iframe or JavaScript code that can be pasted into your CMS or blog platform.

4. Experiment with Facebook Ads

Nonprofits have had mixed results with Facebook Ads. Large non-profits with high brand recognition tend to have good return on investment (ROI) because most people already know the nonprofit when they see its ad pop up on Facebook, and if they already support or have heard of the organization's work, a "Like" of the Facebook Ad (and thus the nonprofit's Facebook Page) is probable. Small nonprof-its with good regional brand recognition can also do well with Facebook Ads, since ads can be targeted by zip code. Others have had minimal success or none whatsoever. It could be that the ad image or ad title was boring, or that they didn't target their ad correctly (age, gender, education level, and so on). That said, if only to understand the pulse of the Facebook community better, your nonprofit should consider experimenting with $50 to $100 worth of Facebook Ads to see if they produce any positive results for your nonprofit. Be sure to set realistic expectations, and do some Google searches on the subject first. In 2010, a study by Webtrends revealed that each new fan acquired through Facebook Ads costs an average of $1.07, so $100 in Facebook Ads may produce only 100 new fans. You'll have to do some cost-benefit analysis to decide whether it is worth the investment to experiment, and if you decide to move forward, know that humorous images tend to produce the best results.

5. Utilize Facebook Events

Nonprofits that regularly host fundraising events and conferences can use the Facebook "Events" app to create event pages that allow people to RSVP directly on Facebook. An app created by Facebook, it comes preinstalled on all Facebook Pages under "Edit Page > Apps > Events." To create an event, simply upload an image for the event (it need not be square) and the event information. You'll notice right away that you cannot use the "Select Guests" function to invite your fans; you can invite only your personal friends on Facebook. That's why you need to be sure to make the event public because the only way you can promote your Facebook Events is by posting the event page in status updates and updates, and by featuring your events on an "Events" tab on your Facebook Page. You also want to be sure to post status updates on your event page's wall. Doing so pulls up the avatar of your nonprofit's Facebook Page, thus increasing the possibility of your getting new fans if you promote your Facebook Events on your website, blog, e-newsletter, and so on. Finally, Facebook Events take only a few minutes to create and manage, but they do not allow registration or payment processing, so they tend to work best for free events, such as protests or meetings. That said, if your event does require registration and payment, post a link to your website where people can register and pay under "More Info." For an example of Facebook Events, see the Facebook Page of the Special Olympics of Northern California at facebook.com/sonorcal.

FIVE STATUS UPDATE CONTENT IDEAS FOR NONPROFITS

Now that you know how to post a status update on Facebook, the next question is, what should you post on Facebook? For the most part, fundraising pitches are ignored, as is press release–like content. In general, tone and subject matter should be timely and personal, and should have a more casual tone than what you write and present in Web 1.0 communications.

1. Success Stories

Your fans want to hear and see that your nonprofit is making progress. Success stories are guaranteed to elicit thumbs ups. With seemingly so much bad news being thrown around the Web on a daily basis, a feel-good story from your nonprofit can work wonders on the psyches of your fans. Keep in mind that most people will only skim the story, so keep it short and positive.

2. Photos

People love photos that tell a story. They want to see the people and places that make up your nonprofit and its work. Whether you post a link to a Flickr slideshow or directly upload your photos from events and campaigns to Facebook, sharing photos with your fans regularly should be a top priority.

3. Videos

Videos help your nonprofit tell its story. If they are done well, they can elicit strong feelings of support and empathy. Of course, you want to share videos created by your nonprofit, but sharing well-produced, powerful videos created by others that speak directly to your nonprofit's mission is also a best practice. Ideally, you should share videos with your fans at least two or three times a month.

4. Breaking News

Social media is driven by breaking news. The 24-hour news cycle has dramatically changed the way people digest and respond to news. In many cases, an event that happened three or four days ago is old news and just does not garner a response on social media. Therefore, today's social media managers need to have a voracious appetite for monitoring breaking news so that they can share it quickly with their communities. That's one of the reasons why blogging is so important in social media: it allows your nonprofit to respond to or share breaking news quickly.

On Facebook, you can either link to the breaking news story directly (for example, sharing a *New York Times* story) or write a few paragraphs about the story in a blog post, then share it on Facebook. The benefit of the latter is obvious. Rather than directing your Facebook fans to the *New York Times* website, you direct them to your blog, complete with your nonprofit's branding.

5. Calls to Action

Calls to action can help motivate your fans to donate, sign online petitions, participate in e-mail campaigns, or sign up to attend events. They are especially effective when they are tied to breaking news. Your fans care about your nonprofit and its mission or they wouldn't have liked your nonprofit in the first place, and sometimes all they need is for you to ask in order to become mobilized and inspired to take action.

FACEBOOK COMMUNITY PAGES?

The purpose of Facebook Community Pages, launched in April 2010, is still a mystery to this day. Most nonprofits don't even know that they have a community page on Facebook, but odds are that they do. A community page is created automatically when individuals go into their personal profiles and "Edit Profile" to add their education and work, philosophy, arts and entertainment, sports, and activities and interests. For example, if you or a work colleague have edited your personal profile and added your nonprofit's name under "Employer," then you've created a community page for your nonprofit. If your nonprofit has a Wikipedia page, then Facebook automatically pulls the logo image and information directly from your Wikipedia page into your community page.

Now, on the one hand, community pages are useful in that they aggregate all the content published on Facebook that is associated with your name under "Related Posts." Once you find your community page, you can use it to monitor what people are saying about your nonprofit on Facebook. On the other hand, community pages sometimes trump your nonprofit's official Facebook Page in Facebook searches. That means that if someone searches for your nonprofit on Facebook, the community page sometimes pops up first, and quite often the official Facebook Page won't show up at all unless the searcher selects "See More Results." Thus, many people are liking the community page instead of the official Facebook Page, which of course, after years of trying to build a Facebook community, annoys a great number of Facebook admins.

To find your nonprofit's community page, first go to "Edit Profile" and then select "Education and Work" to see if you have inadvertently created a community page. If not, then search inside of Facebook to see if any pages pop up with your nonprofit's name that don't appear to be your official Facebook Page. However, community pages sometimes do not appear in searches if you are the admin of the official Facebook Page, so you may need to log in to someone else's Facebook account to find your nonprofit's community page. Once you find it, "Like" it and update your Wikipedia page if necessary. Other than that, the purpose of community pages is unknown, and that's all you can do. Many admins hope that they either quietly disappear or evolve to become more useful.

FINAL WORDS:
HAVE REALISTIC EXPECTATIONS

Creating and managing a Facebook Page is a must for all nonprofits, but it's important to understand that the Facebook Page tool set itself is quite limited. Although Facebook has helped fuel revolutions (literally), this was not done through the use of the Facebook Page tool set. It was the people themselves, organizing and communicating with their friends and family on Facebook, who did it. The personal connections and the personal profile functionality and tool set are still

Facebook's greatest strength. As a marketing tool, quite honestly there's been a lot of hype about Facebook Pages over the years that has set up many nonprofits for disappointment. They are often surprised by how difficult it is to build a fan base on Facebook, and the truth is that it just doesn't happen unless you integrate your Facebook Page into your Web 1.0, Web 2.0, and Web 3.0 campaigns. That said, as long as you have realistic expectations, continue to diversify your brand online, and have the patience to allow your Facebook Page community to grow steadily and slowly, then the ROI of Facebook will reveal itself and grow exponentially in numbers and power over time.

Nonprofit Examples of Excellence

- Humane Society of the United States: facebook.com/humanesociety

- Human Rights Watch: facebook.com/humanrightswatch

- Operation Homefront: facebook.com/operationhomefront

- Pancreatic Cancer Action Network: facebook.com/jointhefight

- Survival International: facebook.com/survival

Google This!

- ❏ Facebook.com/nonprofitorgs

- ❏ Checkfacebook.com

- ❏ Social media millennials

- ❏ Movie the social network

- ❏ Allfacebook.com

- ❏ Facebook.com/help

- ❏ Facebook.com/facebookpages

- ❏ Facebook advertising revenue

- ❏ Facebook news feed algorithm

- ❏ Developers.facebook.com

- ❏ Facebook like boxes

- ❏ Facebook like buttons

- ❏ Is facebook advertising worth it?

- ❏ Facebook.com/insights

- ❏ Facebook events: creating and editing an event, and event privacy

- ❏ Meetup facebook tab app

- ❏ How to: create custom iframe tabs on your nonprofit's facebook page

- ❏ How to: use facebook questions for your nonprofit

- ❏ How to: update your nonprofit's wikipedia page

TWITTER AND TWITTER APPS

We've been so impressed with how easy it is to find people on Twitter who care about causes and making an impact in their communities, both online and off. By paying attention to what volunteers and other volunteer organizations are discussing on Twitter—and by responding and engaging with them—we've been able to make many spontaneous and serendipitous connections with individuals and organizations that likely never would have occurred otherwise.

—*Jessica Kirkwood, vice president, interactive strategy, Points of Light Institute & HandsOn Network*

THE BIG PICTURE: MICROBLOGGING

The explosion of microblogging through "Tweets" has changed Web communication forever. Language purists would say that this has been a change for the worse. Technologists and youth argue that you can't stop progress. Nonprofit communicators are somewhere in the middle. In the brave new world of online communications and fundraising, almost everything that most nonprofit communicators have learned over the last 20 years doesn't work on Twitter and Facebook, and although these people may initially resist the change, they will have to adapt if they are to stay relevant in their careers. Communicating messages in short bursts of information, even if they are sometimes grammatically incorrect, is an acquired and valuable skill that is useful in today's online society and economy.

Now used by over two hundred million people worldwide, Twitter is the best known and most used microblogging platform. However, very few people instinctively "get" Twitter from day one. Most nonprofit communicators learn how to microcommunicate effectively through a process of trial and error over a period of months, or perhaps even years. Mastering Twitter takes time and the willingness to experiment and go against almost everything you learned in Web 1.0 communications and fundraising. Twitter is both more complicated and more fascinating than it appears; it is a community in which success is earned and rarely guaranteed.

INTRODUCTION TO TWITTER PROFILES

In 2010, Twitter began rebranding itself as an information network rather than a social network. The reality is that there is very little socializing on Twitter. Most Twitterers are sharing information about themselves, building a brand, or using Twitter as a breaking news source. The best Twitterers do attempt to connect with people and personalities via tweets, "Retweets," and "Mentions" of 140 characters or less, but the social networking aspect of Twitter is minimal compared to Facebook's. That's a good thing. Facebook and Twitter are completely different tools, with their own unique tool sets, communities, and etiquette. When they are used correctly and with intention, both sites can be very useful for nonprofits.

Whereas on Facebook you need a personal profile in order to create a page for your nonprofit, on Twitter there is no difference. A Twitter Profile can be a person or a brand. As a starting point, nonprofits should create an organizational profile for their nonprofit, such as Twitter.com/NWF. If you discover after a few months of tweeting that Twitter is a good fit for your nonprofit, then you can create additional profiles for campaigns or individual staff members.

To create a Twitter Profile for your nonprofit, go to twitter.com/signup, enter your nonprofit's name in the "Name" field, and then enter your username (which then becomes your Twitter vanity URL), e-mail, and password. Remember that your usernames on Twitter, Facebook, YouTube, Foursquare, and other networks should be the same across all sites, if possible. After you have created your account, go to "Settings > Profile," upload a square version of your nonprofit's avatar, and enter your nonprofit's location, its website address, and a "bio" of your nonprofit's work of 160 characters or less. Also, under "Settings > Account," do not protect your tweets unless you are using Twitter to create a closed community. Otherwise, it's pointless to be on Twitter as a nonprofit if your tweets are protected.

Finally, under "Settings > Account," add a location to your tweets, unless you work at home. In that case, err on the side of caution and do not associate your tweets with your home address. Tweet location comes into play in mobile technology, where users can "View Tweets Nearby," and in third-party Twitter apps that utilize geolocation technology. Enabling location results in more exposure for your nonprofit, but you'll want to make sure that you protect your personal privacy when you're utilizing Twitter's geolocation service (or any geolocation service, for that matter).

Until you have completed all these steps and sent out your first tweet, do not start "Following" others. Many nonprofits immediately start following hundreds of profiles on Twitter, hoping to get some new followers in return, but unless you've followed all the steps given here, your debut on Twitter will be a huge flop. You are 90 percent less likely to be followed in return if you leave your website field or bio blank because many Twitterers will think you are a spammer and will not follow you back. First impressions are very important on Twitter. Make sure yours speaks to your nonprofit, not like a Twitter spammer!

ELEVEN TWITTER BEST PRACTICES FOR NONPROFITS

Most people are not natural-born Twitterers. Even the best social media managers often go through an initial period of experimentation, puzzlement, and frustration as they try to figure out how Twitter works. Some will get it within a few weeks (consider your nonprofit very lucky if that is the case for you), and others will need months for Twitter to click. Unfortunately, many nonprofits abandon Twitter much sooner than they should. There is an ebb and flow to Twitter—a community pulse just underneath the surface of all the millions of tweets that may not be apparent right away. Give it time, and do not rush to judgment. If the Web and mobile technology continue on their current path, having a Twitter community that you can tap into when you need it will be very important in your overall Web strategy in the long run.

1. Find Your Twitter Voice—Have Personality and Build Community

Most nonprofits get on Twitter and immediately start pushing out content about their programs, events, and fundraising campaigns. That's interesting for only a tweet or two, and then it starts to get boring to your followers. If you don't take your twittering beyond the level of push marketing, your followers will start to tune you out or "Unfollow" you. Discovering what kind of content and tone your followers respond to is admittedly a lot easier said than done, but your return on investment (ROI) will be minimal at best if you don't strategically work toward the goal of finding your Twitter voice from the very beginning.

The best nonprofit Twitter voices have personality. They have character. They're friendly. They share opinions and contribute to discussions on Twitter. There's absolutely no doubt among their followers that there is a real human being behind the Twitter avatar. The best nonprofit Twitterers will also engage their followers, send out a wide variety of content (including photos and videos), and unequivocally resist the temptation to automate their tweets or direct messages. Your followers have no interest in following or engaging with bots. They want authenticity. Always remember that the power of social media is not in the tools themselves; rather, it's in the human being using them. This is nowhere more apparent than in the Twitterverse.

Through a process of trial and error over weeks or months, you will discover what works and what doesn't in terms of content and tone. Your ultimate goal should be to inspire action and reaction from your followers. Those responses can range from simply reading your tweet, to clicking through a link posted in your tweet, to retweeting your tweet to their followers. If your nonprofit gets on Twitter and does not notice any sort of response within the first few weeks, then it is time to expand your ideas on what your nonprofit should tweet about.

When you've found your voice, you'll know it. The degree to which you can feel the pulse of your community at your fingertips will vary from day to day, but you will begin to get a sense that it is there and that your followers are listening. The proof will be seen in increased website and blog traffic, mentions, and retweets. Once you have found your voice, the Twitterverse will start to take notice, and your follower base will begin to grow—slowly at first, then exponentially over time. Twitter is not for everyone, but for those who find that it is a fit for their personalities and their nonprofit, it will become an integral part of their daily routine.

2. Track Your Links!

One of the fastest ways to find your Twitter voice is to use a third-party Twitter app, such as Bit.ly or Ow.ly, to track your links. These free tools shrink long links, allowing you more characters for tweeting, and provide useful statistics on how many people clicked on your links. When you are using one of these tools, it becomes clear very quickly whether anyone is clicking on your links, and if no one is doing so, then it's time to try tweeting different content because no clicks means that no one is listening to you on Twitter. Twitterers who do not track their tweeted links are tweeting blindly and, more often than not, incorrectly.

3. Don't Tweet Only Your Own Content

Tweeting only about your nonprofit is boring. Large national and international nonprofits that produce a lot of Twitter-worthy content can sometimes get away with tweeting only about their blog, their news, their events, and their videos, but the vast majority of nonprofits will need to tweet a wide variety of content from sources outside of their organization to keep their Twitter community engaged and growing.

As the Twitterer for your nonprofit, you'll need to mix it up. Tweet articles or blog posts from your favorite newspapers, bloggers, and partner organizations. If the tweet is a good read or is useful, then the fact that you tweeted it reflects well upon your nonprofit and increases the likelihood of reciprocal mentions and retweets. The best Twitterers make it a part of their daily routine to monitor and tweet breaking news that is relevant to their nonprofit. Through tracking mentions, retweets, and click-throughs, they discover over time what kind of content works for their nonprofit on Twitter and what doesn't. Most likely, the recipe for success will be a wide variety of content from many sources mixed with your own. As a general rule, out of every ten tweets, only one should be a direct request, such as subscribe to our e-newsletter, make a donation, like us on Facebook, or something similar.

4. Retweet and Reply Often

Retweet unto others as you would have them retweet unto you is the Golden Rule of Twitter. The more your nonprofit promotes others through retweets and replies, the more your nonprofit will in turn get retweeted and mentioned. Strategically speaking, one of your primary goals on Twitter should be to earn retweets and mentions by others because this is the fastest way to grow your follower base. If your tweets are never retweeted or your profile is never mentioned, then you will remain in Twitter obscurity, relegated to some remote corner of the Twitterverse where your nonprofit will rarely get exposed to potential new followers.

So, how do you get retweeted and mentioned? Primarily by retweeting and replying to others. Generosity is respected and appreciated on Twitter, and even if those that you retweet or reply to do not reciprocate the favor, others will. Twitter is a fascinating real-time example of good karma in technology. What you tweet out eventually comes back to you. Once you get into your flow, find your Twitter voice, and begin to experience your mentions and follower base growing on a consistent daily basis, good Twitter karma can't be denied.

Another way to get retweeted and mentioned, of course, is to tweet interesting content related to breaking news and trending topics that people want to share on Twitter. Again, knowing what kind of content to tweet and when is a big part of finding your Twitter voice. Also, inspirational quotes and powerful statistics related to your organization's mission have high retweet appeal. Definitely make quotes and stats a regular part of your tweeting routine.

Although this is confusing, it must be noted at this point that there are two styles of retweeting on Twitter. The first way is to simply select the "Retweet" icon at the bottom of a tweet. Twitter then automatically shares the tweet with your followers exactly as it was tweeted by the original Twitterer. The second way, known as "old-school retweeting," is to copy and paste the content of the tweet, select the "Reply" icon, and then put an "RT" in front of the tweet, such as:

> RT @pewresearch About 10,000 baby boomers will turn 65
> today. 10,000 more will do so every day for the next 19 years.

While the first method seems appealing, the truth is that it negatively affects your retweet strategy because it posts the original
Twitterer's avatar, not yours, to the timeline. Your followers are accustomed to seeing your avatar and can become slightly annoyed if they
see in their timeline avatars of profiles that they are not following. It's
subtle, but it is enough to make some people unfollow you. The
Twitterverse has never fully embraced the automatic retweet function.
Twitterers prefer the old-school retweets. In addition, automatic
retweets are not listed in mentions, so they are often not acknowl-
edged or even seen by the original Twitterer, making the likelihood of
reciprocity extremely unlikely.

However, automatic retweets do increase your generosity score.
They are the highest expression of selfless tweeting on Twitter, and in
the nonprofit community, that is valued and respected. The magic formula that most maximizes good Twitter karma for your nonprofit is
an average of 80 percent old-school retweeting and 20 percent automatic retweeting, with at least 25 percent of your total tweets being
retweets or replies. Confused? That's OK. You will be in the beginning, but once you begin to experiment with retweeting and replying,
and thus become a better Twitterer, this will make sense because
you'll experience the results yourself. You just need to be willing to go
against everything that traditional marketing has taught you in order
to make Twitter work for your nonprofit. Retweet and reply often!

5. Follow on a 1:1 Ratio

This is another hard concept for some nonprofits. Many people find
following hundreds or even thousands of Twitterers to be overwhelming, but from a strategic communications point of view, you
have nothing to lose and everything to gain by following on a 1:1
ratio—meaning that if you have 1,000 followers, then you should follow 1,000 Twitterers in return. Since Twitter's beginning, studies of

Twitter by HubSpot and others have revealed that this is the magic formula for growing your follower base consistently and steadily over time. Why does the 1:1 ratio work best on Twitter?

- *You're likely to get more followers if people see that you follow in return.* People want to be followed on Twitter. If you don't follow others, your follower base will grow more slowly.

- *People cannot message you directly if you are not following them.* It's a bit of a snub when you want to message someone directly in response to his tweet, but when you visit his profile, you see that there's no option to send a direct message because he is not following you in return.

- *People are less likely to mention or retweet you if they think you'll never retweet or mention them.* You see their tweets only if you follow them, so if you are not following others, you are just broadcasting on Twitter. That can work for some large media outlets, but not for most nonprofits. Your goal should be to build community and momentum on Twitter, and it's pretty much impossible to do that if you are not following and listening to others.

- *People will get an e-mail saying that your nonprofit is now following them.* If a Twitterer has configured her account to receive e-mail notifications, then she will get an e-mail from Twitter saying that your nonprofit is now following her. That builds your brand recognition.

- *Some people will think that you are an egotist.* Following only a small number of people subtly sends a message of exclusivity, which works only for rock stars, celebrities, and large media outlets, and even then it is a little annoying that they take their tweeting and following so seriously. Narcissism is a huge turn-off on Twitter, especially in the nonprofit sector. Humility, commitment to service, and generosity are the qualities to be embraced and nurtured.

Following on a 1:1 ratio will require more time and effort from your nonprofit, but you get out of Twitter what you put into Twitter. Paying more attention to who is following you and following the same number of people in return is an advanced strategy on Twitter. That doesn't mean that you follow everyone who follows you! Weed out the spammers. For every spammer you don't follow in return, follow a foundation or nonprofit blogger that isn't currently following you. Hopefully, they will follow back.

Finally, never go out and follow hundreds or thousands of people when you have only a handful of followers. People will then think that you are a spammer (or desperate) and will not follow you in return. Slow and steady is what works on Twitter. A lot of nonprofits make mistakes from day one on Twitter, then wonder why it doesn't work for them and give up. Twitter is not for everyone, but it can be very powerful as long as you learn the etiquette.

6. Create "Lists" to Organize the Chaos and Build Partnerships

Assuming that you are now following hundreds or even thousands of people on Twitter, creating "Lists" allows you to organize your favorite Twitterers into groups. Rather than having to browse for their tweets among the thousands in your home view, you can simply add them to a Twitter List in order to filter their tweets into a more visually manageable format. To create a Twitter List, simply go to "Lists > Create a list." If you choose to make your lists public, make sure you are consistent in formatting your lists (all lowercase letters, for example), because lists are featured on your profile and are viewable and followable by others.

Why make your lists public? To build partnerships on Twitter. Create lists for supporters, donors, volunteers, foundations, allies, chapters, staff, and so on. Being listed is similar to getting a thumbs up or like on Facebook. It makes people feel good. Many nonprofits make the mistake of approaching list making with the idea of creating lists that others will want to follow, but in a Twitterverse loaded with millions of lists, that's rare. Rather, use lists to express generosity and goodwill. As with the laws of mentions and retweets, the more you list others, the more you tend to get listed, and being listed increases your credibility as a Twitterer. Underneath the flood of millions of tweets is an etiquette based on generosity and reciprocity. Unfortunately, many nonprofits never dig deep enough to understand or experience this uniquely Twitter phenomenon.

7. Use Hashtags Strategically and with Authenticity

Hashtags allow Twitterers to discuss issues and events on Twitter in real time. They also function as a means to organize tweets, spread information, and find new followers. A hashtag is expressed by placing a hash symbol ("#") in front of a topic in a tweet, such as #AIDS or #fundraising. Hashtags are then automatically hyperlinked within Twitter so that users can click the hashtag link to view all other tweets that have the same hashtag.

In the early days of Twitter, there was no search function, so Twitterers had to use hashtags in order to converse on Twitter and find others with similar interests. Today, a simple search inside of Twitter fulfills that purpose, but hashtags have continued to be an integral part of the Twitterverse, although their primary function has changed. Hashtags now serve as a means for real-time discussion and reporting during events and as tags to gain or discover new followers.

Hashtags are confusing to many new Twitterers, but as with most new online tools, the best way to learn is just to start browsing hashtags and experimenting with your own. That having been said, there is hashtag etiquette to follow to avoid being perceived as a hashtag spammer. Less is more! Any given tweet should not have more than one or two hashtags, and not every tweet should include hashtags. This is an example of hashtag spam:

> One in four #mammals on #earth now at risk of #extinction due to #overpopulation and loss of #habitat. Re: #biodiversity #wildlife

It's clear that this Twitterer is using hashtags mostly to gain new followers and probably isn't browsing the hashtags themselves. Too many hashtags clutter and fragment hashtag conversations and almost always annoy the Twitterverse. Your hashtag mantra should be "authenticity over marketing."

8. Tweet Four to Six Times per Day

The lifespan of a tweet is about 90 minutes. Most people browse only tweets in their timeline in real time. It's rare that a tweet that you posted last week gets traction. If you have someone on staff who enjoys Twitter (ideally, that person should be your social media manager) and has a voracious appetite for news, then that person should be logging in to Twitter and tweeting four to six times per day. Tweets need to be spaced out throughout the day to accommodate people's different time schedules, especially if you are a national or international nonprofit. Twitter is most active from 9 a.m. to 12 p.m. in any given time zone, so tweet accordingly. You can use HootSuite to preschedule tweets to go out overnight if you are trying to reach international audiences. That said, never send your daily four to six tweets all at once! Some nonprofits and personalities on Twitter tweet all day long, sometimes posting 20 tweets or more, but they can pull it off because their Twitter voice is engaging rather than annoying.

Many nonprofits are overwhelmed by the thought of tweeting four to six times per day. If time and resources are an issue, then post only one tweet per day or every other day, but just understand that you get out of Twitter what you put into it. It's very difficult to build momentum on Twitter with sporadic tweeting. Four to six tweets per day is enough to have a consistent presence on Twitter, but not so many that your followers get annoyed and unfollow you. It's a fine line, and it varies a bit depending upon your nonprofit's mission, programs, and size. Only through trial and error and time spent will you find the right balance unique to your nonprofit.

9. Use "Favorites" to Bookmark Future Retweets and Feature Your Most Important Tweets!

Many times you'll come across a tweet in your timeline that you think would be valuable to retweet to your followers, but the timing is not right at that particular moment. Favoriting such tweets is an easy way to bookmark them for future retweeting. Also, using the favorites function to archive your most important tweets gives them added exposure to your followers and helps make Twitter more manageable and productive. A small percentage of your most successful tweets should be reposted periodically, and favoriting the original makes it easy to locate that tweet when that time comes. Although most Twitterers don't use the favorites function, they should. Once it becomes clear to you how to use the function and how valuable it is, it is likely to become a daily part of your Twitter routine.

10. Use Twitter to Build Your E-newsletter List

Sometimes all you have to do is ask! It's amazing how willing and eager many Twitterers are to support your nonprofit if you simply ask them to. This can be a simple "Please RT!" or a pitch to join your e-newsletter list. While asking for donations via tweets tends to fall on deaf ears, asking people to subscribe to your e-newsletters does not. Remember, the vast majority of online donations come directly from asks in e-newsletters, so to increase your social media fundraising ROI, turn those followers into e-newsletter subscribers. Every couple of weeks, send out a time-sensitive tweet letting people know that your nonprofit is "Sending out an e-newsletter tomorrow, and if you want to receive a copy, please subscribe!" Of course, provide a link where they can automatically subscribe themselves. Quite often a "Thank You!" in the tweet helps increase your opt-in rate. However, less is more. Ask your followers to subscribe to your e-newsletter only two or three times a month, but most definitely do ask.

11. Design Your Twitter Profile to Match Your Organization's Online Branding

At the very least, nonprofits need to log in to their Twitter profile, go to "Settings > Design > Change design colors," and enter the numeric values of the colors of their avatar. Call your designer and ask for the numeric values of your Web colors if you need to, or use the 4096 Color Wheel (Google it!) to guesstimate your colors. Even better, design a simple, custom background image for your Twitter Profile. Make sure that it includes your logo, tagline, and website address. Inspirational quotes and statistics usually get your followers' attention as well. If your nonprofit is utilizing text-to-give technology, definitely include your text-to-give keyword and short code pitch. The background image size should be 1,280 pixels wide by 800 pixels in height (100 pixels = 1 inch). Once the image has been designed, simply go to "Settings > Design > Change background image" and upload your custom background. The National Wildlife Federation (@NWF) and charity: water (@charitywater) regularly use custom background images.

ELEVEN TWITTER APPS FOR NONPROFITS

The rise of Twitter has resulted in the proliferation of thousands of third-party Twitter apps. From simple URL stat trackers to full-fledged micro-giving and cause communities, the Twitterverse includes much more than just what's available at Twitter.com. Here are 11 useful Twitter apps for nonprofits, but a good nonprofit Twitterer will always be on the lookout for new Twitter apps to experiment with. Be sure to create an account at oneforty.com (an online database of third-party Twitter apps) and sign up for e-mail alerts about new and useful Twitter apps.

1. Bit.ly

Bit.ly allows users to shorten, share, and track links (URLs). It provides detailed statistical data on how many people click on your links and retweet your links, at what time of day, what country they are located in, and even how many people shared your links on Facebook. HubSpot has studied and reported that Bit.ly links are much more likely to get retweeted on Twitter than any other link format, so it's worth noting that Bit.ly is integrated into most third-party Twitter and social media dashboards.

2. TwentyFeet

TwentyFeet.com provides an additional set of useful Twitter analytics that Bit.ly does not. You can sign up to review weekly, monthly, or quarterly reports on how many new followers, retweets, and mentions you've earned, as well as how many times your nonprofit's Twitter Profile was listed on Twitter. You can track one Twitter and Facebook account for free, and then add additional Twitter, Facebook, and YouTube accounts for $2.49 each per year. Best of all, TwentyFeet allows integration with your Bit.ly account thus allowing you to monitor all your statistics in one place.

3. Twtpoll

Twtpoll.com allows you to create simple multiple-choice polls that can be easily tweeted and tracked. You can embed images or videos inside your polls, and if you upgrade to the premium version, you can also create surveys, get access to widgets, and have Twitter and Facebook comments integrated into your polls. Most nonprofits will probably use Twtpoll only three or four times a year, but it is a tool that can add some creativity to Twitter campaigns. Also, if the Twtpoll becomes popular, it can help your nonprofit get more exposure on Twitter, which is likely to result in new followers.

A good practice is to create Twtpolls related to breaking news that will have mass appeal (Do you think Congress should have passed such-and-such bill?) or to seek advice about your campaigns or marketing efforts (What should we name our new blog?). A "Poll of the

Month," and then reporting on the results of all 12 polls at the end of the year, is usually a hit with your supporters both within and outside of the Twitterverse. Twtpolls also work very well in mobile browsers and should occasionally be sent to your group text messaging list. After a few Twtpolls, you'll get a better sense of what works and what doesn't and how often to create and promote them. The most important aspect of Twtpolls, and really of all third-party Twitter apps, is to do something different.

4. TwitPic, TwitVid, or yfrog

In addition to or in the place of Twitter's native photo and video sharing tool, nonprofits can use TwitPic.com to share photos on Twitter in real time from your smartphone or tablet, via e-mail, or directly from TwitPic.com. Ideal for reporting while on location, TwitPic-related apps upload your images to the TwitPic server and then generate short URLs that can be inserted into tweets directly from your smartphone with a simple tap or two. By default, using TwitPic automatically creates a profile using the data in your Twitter account (twitpic.com/photos/nonprofitorgs) that archives all your photos for future viewing and sharing. Similar in design and functionality, TwitVid.com hopes to be for video what TwitPic is for photos. TwitVid users can also upload videos directly from their smartphone or tablet, or from a Webcam on their computer. Videos can then be shared on Twitter with just a few clicks. Again, by default, simply using TwitVid creates a profile using the data in your Twitter account (twitvid.com/videos/nonprofitorgs) that archives all your videos. Finally, unlike TwitPic and TwitVid, yfrog enables nonprofits to upload and share both photos and videos in real time. TwitPic and TwitVid are the most popular photo-sharing services outside of Twitter, but that could easily change. Before you decide which service to use, spend 30 minutes experimenting with all three and then decide. Mobile communications and real-time reporting will play a very important role in nonprofit communications in the future, so don't rush your decision.

For social media managers on the go, sharing short videos from events and conferences will increasingly become a part of their job description. As smartphone and tablet technology evolves and improves, so will video quality and editing options. Experimenting with services like TwitVid and yfrog now could pay off significantly a few years down the road. Recent studies by Quantcast and Morgan Stanley predict that mobile Internet traffic will overtake desktop traffic by 2015, and a good portion of that traffic will be mobile video. Learning how to record, report, interview, upload, and share videos is a skill set that may take a few years to master, so now would be a good time to start if you haven't already.

5. Twibbon

Twibbon.com allows nonprofits to create "Twibbons" for their nonprofit brand or cause that Twitterers can easily overlay on their own Twitter avatars to show support for the nonprofit or cause. Most nonprofits use their logo as their Twibbon image, but you can also design and launch Twibbons for specific campaigns, such as a red ribbon for #WorldAIDSDay. Creating a Twibbon can be a bit tedious. There are a number of steps to go through, and you have to be able to design a Twibbon using photo editing and graphic design software that allows transparent backgrounds. You may need to hire a graphic designer for 30 minutes of work, but it's worth the time and effort. Twibbons are useful on Twitter, Facebook, and location-based communities like Foursquare and Gowalla, especially if you have numerous staff members utilizing social media. The more staff members and supporters you have out there on the Web using your nonprofit's Twibbon, the more visually recognizable and powerful your brand will become.

6. TweetMeme

TweetMeme.com primarily serves as a portal to popular tweets organized into channels ranging from comedy to technology, but it also provides some very handy retweet buttons that can be easily added to your blog or website. Users sign up for TweetMeme using their Twitter login, and then are given access to code for the button that can be easily copied and pasted. Twitter also provides code for its own official "Tweet" buttons, but the TweetMeme retweet button has an advantage over Twitter's button in that you can add a retweet button to any WordPress.com blog by simply inserting the text "[tweetmeme]" at the beginning of each blog post. Unfortunately, it's harder than it should be to add retweet buttons to many blog platforms, so the [tweetmeme] function is a great service.

7. Act.ly

Act.ly allows your nonprofit to create Twitter-based petitions. If your nonprofit is an activist or advocacy organization, Act.ly is definitely worth experimenting with. You can petition politicians or corporations that have profiles on Twitter to take action on legislation or an issue, and supporters simply tweet the petition to sign on. Each tweet mentions the politician or corporation and prompts the supporter to follow your nonprofit on Twitter. If your petition has mass appeal, it can result in hundreds or possibly thousands of new followers for your nonprofit and flood the targeted politician or corporation with mentions demanding action.

8. Cinchcast

Cinchcast.com allows users to easily share audio messages online that you have recorded using the microphone on your computer or smartphone. Once uploaded, the audio files are given a short Cinchcast URL that can be easily shared on Twitter or Facebook with followers, who simply click on to listen to your message over their computer speakers. A social media manager with a little creativity could think of numerous ways to use this tool, such as interviewing people at events (conferences, fundraisers, protests, and so on); recording famous quotes, songs, or animal sounds; or even having

Cinchcast messages from staff members integrated into your website or blog. Alternatively, there is Chirbit.com.

9. Twtvite

Twtvite.com allows your nonprofit to easily create "Tweetups" for events. In just a few clicks, you can create an event invitation, known as a Twtvite, and easily invite all your Twitter followers, who then RSVP by sending a tweet to their followers. Non-Twitter members and Facebookers can also RSVP. In addition, the service allows you to create a Twtvite Group for future event management and also print guest lists and name tags. For a small fee, you can upgrade to the premium service, which allows custom branding, online payments, and ticket services.

10. Social Good Apps and Portals

Social media for social good is very popular with technology entrepreneurs and has resulted in an explosion of third-party Twitter apps that serve nonprofits. Some will make it; some won't. Finding a revenue model that enables the company to be sustainable while at the same time not being too aggressive with advertising or having high donation processing fees is a challenge to social entrepreneurs. Your nonprofit should research and participate in sites like TwitCause.com, TwitChange.com, GiveaTweet.com, RainmakerApp.com, BroadCause .com, and Tweenate.org, but be aware that their long-term sustainability is unpredictable.

11. Twitter Mosaic

Twitter Mosaic (sxoop.com/twitter) allows you to create an image with a mosaic of your Twitter followers' avatars. Useful for Web campaigns, Twitter Mosaic also provides the ability to create T-shirts that include your nonprofit's Twitter name and your mosaic of followers.

These T-shirts make great gifts for interns and volunteers, and are a creative way to promote your Twitter account at conferences and other events.

TWITTER FOR FUNDRAISING?

When Twitter first started becoming popular in the nonprofit sector, social good entrepreneurs launched a handful of micro-fundraising services. The best known was TipJoy.com. The Twitterverse was excited about the idea of micro-giving, and nonprofits hoped for a new revenue stream, but the site shut down within a year. Other sites that were similar in purpose followed shortly thereafter. The primary reason that such sites have not survived is that our technology does not yet enable the nonprofit sector to micro-give and micro-fundraise cost-effectively. For example, an online donation of $2 requires, on average, a 35-cent transaction fee plus an additional 3 to 5 percent processing fee on the total donation. Combined, that's close to 20 percent of the donation going to banks and credit card companies—much too high to allow donors and fundraisers to embrace micro-fundraising as a plausible option for nonprofits. Until online social entrepreneurs can find a way to make it financially reasonable to donate online in amounts less than $10, micro-fundraising will struggle to succeed.

That doesn't mean that Twitter can't be useful for your online fundraising campaigns. Indeed, it can be as long as you understand and embrace the very premise of this book—use Web 2.0 tools to complement your Web 1.0 communications and online fundraising strategies. Use Twitter to build your online brand so that your followers visit your website and subscribe to your e-newsletter; then, when they have cash to give, they will choose to respond to your Donate Now campaigns over hundreds of others because they have been engaged and inspired by your tweets. Unless you poll your online donors, it's impossible to track your followers and why they chose your nonprofit to donate to, but online giving has increased significantly since the rise of social media, and is likely to continue to do so as social media becomes more deeply integrated into the Web as a whole. Increasingly, if your nonprofit does not utilize social media, it does not exist to any online donors, or at the very least, it is overshadowed by those nonprofits that do.

HOW TO LAUNCH A TWITTER FUNDRAISING CAMPAIGN

Obstacles to micro-fundraising aside, some nonprofits could be successful using Twitter for fundraising. If your nonprofit has a follower base of at least 5,000, some resources to invest in experimentation, and a celebrity or a major donor to enlist, then it could be worth the time and effort to launch a Twitter fundraising campaign. There are no proven best practices or case studies, but given a green light, a superstar social media manager could launch a Twitter campaign that could result in thousands of dollars in donations and new supporters.

- *Center your campaign around a cause, not around your nonprofit's name.* Social good activists and donors respond well to cause campaigns, such as Stop the Seal Hunt, End Human Trafficking, or Feed the Hungry. Your first step is to craft language for a cause campaign that is relevant to your nonprofit's mission and programs.

- *Launch a microsite or blog for your campaign.* If your campaign is to be retweet-worthy, it needs a unique, Twitter-infused microsite or blog. Graphics should have Twitter iconography, and tweets should be displayed in real time. Make sure your e-newsletter "Subscribe" and "Donate Now" buttons are colorful and prominently featured. Twestival.com is a good example.

- *Create a unique #hashtag for the campaign.* Examples are #StoptheSealHunt, #EndHumanTrafficking, and #FeedTheHungry.

- *Get your #hashtag sponsored.* If you have a major donor or corporate sponsor, ask it to donate $0.25 to $1 every time someone tweets your hashtag. For example, some past campaigns
  on Twitter included Häagen-Dazs donating $1 to UC Davis
  for every mention of #HelpHoneyBees and Kraft Foods
  donating a meal to Feeding America for every mention of
  #KraftFightsHunger.

- *Get your campaign sponsored.* Similarly, La-Z-Boy donated $1
  to Ronald McDonald House Charities for every new follower
  that La-Z-Boy received over a 30-day period. Twitter sponsor-
  ship campaigns have a strong appeal for corporations and
  small businesses because they also help the business build its
  follower base.

- *Create a Twibbon.* YWCA Canada launched a "Rose Campaign"
  to encourage supporters to take action against domestic violence (www.rosecampaign.ca). In addition to sending roses to
  members of Parliament, donating, and copying and pasting
  Web badges, supporters could also "scatter petals" by adding
  a rose Twibbon to their Twitter avatar.

- *Have a start and end date.* A sense of urgency always motivates
  people to take action. A month or so before the launch of your
  campaign, e-mail supporters, blog, tweet, and Facebook about
  the launch date to build momentum and excitement. Once
  your campaign is launched, let people know that the campaign will last only 7 to 30 days, and do a heavy push in the
  last days to get your supporters involved.

- *Make it an annual event.* Like your annual gala or conference,
  your online Twitter campaign should become an annual event.
  Just make sure that you add something new each year, such as
  videos, peer-to-peer fundraising, text-to-give, or tweetups.

FINAL WORDS:
EVERYWHERE A TWEET, TWEET!

Unlike personal Facebook status updates, tweets are public. Anyone can go to Twitter at any time and do a search for what people are saying about what is trending online. That's one of the reasons why the media outlets are so enamored with Twitter. They can embed real-time Twitter feeds directly onto their websites or blogs, and even broadcast tweets live on television without much hesitation over privacy concerns. That slight technical difference between private personal status updates and public tweets gives Twitter an advantage and a higher likelihood of being integrated into emerging communications technologies, such as Internet TV and geolocation services. Soon, we will be seeing tweets everywhere. However, if your nonprofit is not active on Twitter, then we won't be seeing yours. Again, it's a Brave New Web where the most engaged and the earliest to adopt thrive.

Nonprofit Examples of Excellence

- Feeding America: twitter.com/feedingamerica

- Human Rights Campaign: twitter.com/hrc

- Stand Up to Cancer: twitter.com/SU2C

- Wildlife SOS: twitter.com/wildlifesos

- Women for Women International: twitter.com/womenforwomen

Google This!

- ❏ Twitter.com/nonprofitorgs

- ❏ Aworldoftweets.com

- ❏ How to: tweet for an international audience

- ❏ 10 popular hashtags for nonprofits

- ❏ Whatthetrend.com

- ❏ Oneforty.com

- ❏ Klout.com

- ❏ Twibbon.com/nonprofitorgs

- ❏ Hope140.org

YOUTUBE AND FLICKR

Rather than telling your nonprofit's story in one long video, think of it instead as shooting numerous scenes for a movie. Each video is a shorter story that can focus on a specific campaign, program, or achievement—all with their own beginning, middle, and end, but collectively the videos tell the complete story of the nonprofit and its mission.

—*Marianna Moneymaker,*
online outreach and
production, WITNESS

THE BIG PICTURE: STORYTELLING THROUGH VIDEO AND PHOTOS

Nonprofits have been telling their stories of success, sorrow, and outrage through print newsletters, annual reports, and funding appeals for decades. The concept of storytelling is not new to nonprofit communicators and fundraisers. What is still relatively new is the idea of telling those same stories through video on YouTube and photostreams and slideshows on Flickr. In this era of information overload, a well-produced video or emotion-evoking slideshow can often get through to the hearts and minds of your supporters much better than any print article, website news story, or blog post could. Every nonprofit has stories to tell. Your challenge today is to learn how to tell them in new, more colorful, more visual ways.

YouTube and Flickr are the two best-known video and digital photography communities online. Though there are social networking components to both sites, it's rare that a YouTube Channel or Flickr account will result in thousands of new supporters for your nonprofit in the way that Facebook or Twitter could. Rather, YouTube and Flickr offer exceptional tool sets for sharing and distributing your nonprofit's videos and photos that can help your nonprofit better engage the supporters that you already have. With a little tech know-how, commitment, and passion, any nonprofit can tap into the power of storytelling through video and digital photography.

GETTING STARTED WITH VIDEO

The idea of creating videos for your nonprofit may seem daunting, but with the explosion of pocket camcorders and video editing tools in recent years, you'll discover that it is much easier and more affordable than you may realize. Technically, it is not that difficult to create a video. The bigger challenge is to find the person within your organization who has the creativity and the passion necessary to produce videos for your nonprofit. It's not for everyone. There's an art to creating videos that inspire emotion and action on the part of your supporters.

To get started, you'll first need to decide who within your organization will create, edit, and upload videos and then manage your video library. It may not be the communications director or the social media manager. Instead, it may your office manager or program director. The point is to ask around and find the person(s) who is most enthusiastic about the idea. Video creation and editing requires a creative eye and forward thinking. It's ideal if your social media manager can also become your video producer, but his primary job is sharing the videos and integrating them into your Web campaigns.

Ideally, your nonprofit should produce videos on a somewhat regular basis (monthly, for example), but at the very least your nonprofit should work toward achieving a goal of a minimum of three videos per year that tell your nonprofit's most important stories, such as your overall mission, your impact, and your future goals. If there is no one in your organization who both wants to do that and feels that she has the skills and capacity, then you can

- *Recruit a videography intern.* A good idea is to contact the career center at your local university and recruit a junior or senior marketing or arts major as an intern. Most likely he will earn college credit for the internship, so he will want to produce good-quality videos for your nonprofit, both to get a good grade and to build his professional portfolio. Alternatively, you can ask around. There are many budding videographers and filmmakers out there who are looking to make a name for themselves.

- *Use Animoto.* Animoto.com allows you to create videos with digital photos. In reality, they are not actually videos, but rather slideshows set to music. However, Animoto videos can be uploaded to YouTube; consequently, they function like any other YouTube video and can be shared throughout the Web. Animoto Pro is a premium service that is free to nonprofits through their Animoto for a Cause program.

- *Create a "Favorites" channel.* Your nonprofit can have a YouTube Channel without ever actually uploading a video by simply featuring your favorite videos on your channel. Of course, you need to integrate video into your strategic plan eventually, but if you want to get started right away, favoriting videos by partners, organizations, funders, and activists with missions similar to yours is an easy way to do so. For example, the "Nonprofit Organizations YouTube Channel" is a favorite-only channel; see youtube.com/nonprofitorgs.

- *Hire a videographer.* Depending on whom you hire, fees could range from $500 to $5,000 per video. The important thing to keep in mind is that videos rarely go viral. The chance that you or someone you hire will create a video that receives hundreds of thousands of views is minuscule, so invest accordingly.

- *Host a video contest.* Launching and maintaining an annual video contest campaign, complete with prizes and incentives, could be a good investment of your time and resources. It depends on whether you think your supporter base is one that can be successfully tapped to produce videos. Generally, nonprofits related to the arts, education, nature, or youth tend to have the best results with video contest campaigns.

PRODUCING AND EDITING VIDEOS

To begin producing your own videos, you will need to invest in a digital camcorder and editing software. It may be surprising to most nonprofits, but this usually requires an initial investment of only $250 or less. A top-quality point-and-record pocket camcorder costs an average of $150. Video files can be easily downloaded to your computer with just a few clicks. If your budget allows, you may also want to purchase a tripod, a wide-angle lens, and a video light for low-light shooting—purchasing all three can cost as little as $100. The number of low-cost tools available to nonprofits today is truly astounding.

After you have your camera and accessories, you'll need to purchase video editing software for cutting, overlays, text, music, and special effects. A quick Google search will reveal that some of the highest-rated video editing software costs $75 or less. Next, for some of your videos, you will probably need to purchase music. YouTube will mute your videos if you use a song that is under copyright without the explicit permission of the artist. Sites like AudioJungle.com allow you to purchase songs for video background effects for as little as $1 each. Finally, some video production training would be a smart investment. It is likely to save you a lot of time and significantly improve the quality of your videos. Videomaker.com offers a suite of free online tutorials and low-cost Webinars.

Now fully equipped and ready to begin, your chosen videographer(s) needs to create a plan of action. The first priority should be creating promotional videos about your nonprofit and its work, that is, your mission, your impact, and your future goals. The purpose of these videos is primarily to summarize your work. When you are creating these videos, it is important to keep in mind that most video watchers get bored and quit watching within the first 10 seconds if the video does not grab their attention effectively. In general, these videos work best if they are limited to 30 seconds. Your supporters today are very busy and have increasingly shorter attention spans.

Depending upon the creativity and capacity of your videographer(s), there's unlimited potential for your nonprofit to tell its stories with video. In addition to the three promotional videos, here are some additional ideas to help get you started:

- *Document events.* Record sound bites of support from attendees at your annual gala or marathon. Interview people who attend your conferences or protests. Record your journey to Capitol Hill or other destinations. Create a fast-forward montage of community-service events. There's no shortage of possibilities when you are documenting events with video, but when you are recording individuals at these events, you should get their permission to publish the video content. As a general rule of thumb, you can record groups of people legally when they are on public property, but when you are recording and then distributing videos of individuals (at events, on the street, or at your office), it's always best to get them to sign a video release form to avoid worst-case scenarios. That having been said, videos of millions of people are being uploaded to YouTube every day without those people's written permission. Use your best judgment, but err on the side of caution.

- *Give a tour of your office or facilities.* Supporters love to see video tours of your office or facilities. They want to see a face and location behind the avatar. They want to see where the work is done and by whom. Similarly, arts organizations can give video tours of galleries and backstage video passes. Animal shelters can present behind-the-scenes videos of caretaking for animals. Any nonprofit that is a destination (museums, food banks, shelters, schools and universities, religious institutions, parks, clinics, and so on) should record a teaser tour to get people interested and eventually walking through the door.

- *Interview staff members, supporters, or experts.* Sit down for a one-on-one with your executive director or your program staff and give them a 10-question interview. Create videos of supporters talking about why they give or volunteer. Interview experts on topics related to your mission and programs. Think of yourself as a broadcast reporter out in the field conducting interviews.

- *Create montages of video clips with powerful stats or quotes embedded.* Using either photos or short video clips, create an inspirational montage video that features powerful quotes and stats. A good song can make a strong impression and keep people watching. These types of videos do very well on the Social Web and can make a big impact on supporters.

- *Feature beneficiaries of your nonprofit's services.* Supporters appreciate success stories. Interview the people who have benefited from your nonprofit and ask them to share their stories.

- *Document important speeches by staff members.* Often the members of your executive staff will give important speeches and presentations at events and conferences that are worth recording and sharing with supporters who could not attend. Creating these videos is as simple as point and shoot. Introductory and closing slides are the only editing requirements. They don't need to be highly polished. In fact, more often than not, authenticity in video production trumps a highly polished marketing approach.

INTRODUCTION TO YOUTUBE CHANNELS

Launched in 2005 and now owned by Google, YouTube is the world's most popular, highly trafficked online video community. On a daily basis, people on YouTube watch more than three billion videos. In fact, 48 hours of video is uploaded to YouTube every minute. Unlike many other online communities, YouTube's users are incredibly diverse in age, race, class, and location. No matter what type of constituencies your nonprofit serves, odds are that they are active on YouTube in large numbers.

To create a YouTube Channel for your nonprofit, go to youtube.com/create_account. It's important to note that the username you select at this first step will become your YouTube vanity URL, such as youtube.com/nonprofitorgs. It cannot be changed in the future, so reserve wisely! You can hide the birthday and gender information later, so don't fret too much about your nonprofit's age and gender.

During the sign-up process, you will also be prompted to create a Google account. This gets a little confusing, but it could save your nonprofit a lot of hassle in the long run. If you already have a Google account that matches your chosen vanity URL(s) for your YouTube Channel and other online communities, such as google.com/profiles/nonprofitorgs, then log in with that account and complete the sign-up process. If you don't, then go to Gmail.com, create a new Gmail e-mail account to match your preferred username, such as nonprofitorgs@gmail.com, and complete the YouTube sign-up process with your new Gmail e-mail address. YouTube will then create your new YouTube Channel as well as a new Google account for your nonprofit, automatically using your new Gmail username as your new Google account vanity URL. This vanity URL also cannot be changed at a later date. As Google continues to expand its services (especially in the mobile arena), your new Google account could become very important in the branding of your nonprofit. Finally, remember to keep track of all these new accounts and logins on your master login sheet.

ELEVEN YOUTUBE BEST PRACTICES FOR NONPROFITS

For the simple reason that YouTube dwarfs all other video sites in terms of users and traffic, it should be the starting point for your nonprofit's online video campaigns. If you want to expand to other online video communities later (such as Vimeo, yfrog, Viddy, Veoh, and Viddler), then by all means do so. That said, the vast majority of nonprofits aren't aware of all that you can do with a YouTube Channel in terms of design, branding, and community building. The best practices given here highlight the most important functions of a YouTube Channel and, if implemented, can transform your YouTube return on investment (ROI).

1. Use Your Nonprofit's Avatar as Your Profile Picture

Your nonprofit's avatar is very important for branding on YouTube. Your avatar will be displayed on all the channels you subscribe to and become friends with, as well as on the walls of any comments you post. It should be square and include your logo, and it should be the same avatar that you use on your other communities. YouTube is a visual community where avatars trump text or titles, so to maximize brand recognition, never use a photo as your profile picture.

2. Use the Colors of Your Avatar to Design Your Channel

YouTube offers one-click automatic branding for your channel. As with Twitter, you should log in, go to "My Channel > Themes and Colors > Show Advanced Options," and enter the numeric values of the colors of your avatar. Again, these numbers can be provided to you by your graphic designer or guesstimated by using the 4096 Color Wheel.

3. Limit the Description of Your Channel to Your Mission Statement or One Paragraph

People are not on YouTube to read. They are there to watch videos and be entertained and inspired. Don't overwhelm your viewers with unnecessary text. Simply go to "My Channel > Profile > Edit" and enter a brief "Channel Description" and link to your website. Disable most categories that you see there, such as age, movies, schools, and music. Keep your profile section simple.

4. Maximize Your YouTube Search Engine Optimization Using Channel Tags and Video Titles

YouTube is now considered the second largest search engine in the world, behind only Google. To maximize the possibility that your videos turn up in YouTube search results, first go to "My Channel > Settings > Channel Tags" and enter a wide variety of tags that you think potential supporters of your work will search for in YouTube. Obvious tags are nonprofit, organization, your city, your state, and your program areas (environment, homelessness, international development, and so on).

Next, when you are uploading videos to your channel, again add as many tags as possible to each video, give a strong but brief description, and, most important, title the video to optimize your YouTube search engine optimization (SEO). Titles have the strongest impact on YouTube search results after your channel's name, so be clever and creative when titling your videos. For example, an excellent video by the Community Housing Partnership with the title "Inside Looking Out" would probably get much more traffic if it were renamed "Inside Looking Out: Homelessness in San Francisco, California." Another example is a video by Philanthropy Reports with the title "Know Your Sector." The video showcases some interesting stats and data about the nonprofit sector, but it would get much more traffic if it were renamed "Philanthropy Reports: Know Your Nonprofit Sector."

5. Enable Channel and Video Comments

YouTube is much more than simply a place to host your nonprofit's videos. It's a thriving online community. If you don't allow comments on your channel or your videos, then you have cut yourself off from the YouTube community. Unless your nonprofit works on controversial issues like religion, politics, immigration, or abortion and you don't want to have to monitor your comments on a daily basis, enable channel and video comments. The vast majority of the time, the comments will be positive and supportive. For the few that aren't, if they are exceptionally mean-spirited, then simply delete them, block the user, and move on. That said, there are seemingly more mean and grumpy people on YouTube than on any other community. Try not to be too shocked when you experience your first.

6. Display Subscribers and Friends

The more "Subscribers" and "Friends" your nonprofit has, the more exposure you get on YouTube. You are also much more likely to get new subscribers and friend requests if you display subscribers and friends on your channel. The avatars of your subscribers and friends also add some color and personality to your channel, and send the message that your nonprofit is engaged in the YouTube community.

7. Send Friend Requests Weekly

YouTube limits the number of friend requests your nonprofit can send per hour to 28, and you can't send all 28 requests in a row. They have to be spread out over an hour. It can be frustrating, but it's worth setting aside one day each week to send 10 to 20 friend requests. Over time, you want to build a community of a couple of hundred, and eventually thousands, of friends on your YouTube Channel. Like all communities, the larger yours gets, the more it grows exponentially and increases in power.

To begin, search for YouTubers in your area (city, state, or country) and simply send them a friend request. Also, search for YouTubers by issue or cause, and send them friend requests too. It's also good to be friends with your local media on YouTube, and with foundations and funders. It's worth noting that subscribers are much more valuable on YouTube because they see your new videos in their video feeds as you upload them, but having many friends helps increase your avatar visibility within the YouTube community. It's definitely worth 10 minutes a week of your time to send friend requests.

8. Subscribe to Channels Created by Funders and Partners

Subscribing to a channel on YouTube is the highest expression of support on YouTube. Search for and subscribe to channels created by foundations and businesses that fund your nonprofit. If your nonprofit works in partnership with other nonprofits, subscribe to their channels, too. Also, if your nonprofit has numerous chapters, subscribe and send friend requests to all of them. On YouTube, the more you subscribe to others, the more subscribers you get in return. That said, be more selective in your subscribing than in your friending. You want a subscription to mean more than a friendship on YouTube.

9. Sign Up for YouTube's Nonprofit Program

YouTube offers a nonprofit program for legal nonprofits in the United States, Canada, the United Kingdom, and Australia. There is an application process, and take note that nonprofits that are religious or political in nature are excluded from participating in the program. While the application process itself is fast and simple, approval can often take weeks. You can learn more about the application process and program benefits at youtube.com/nonprofits.

10. Integrate Your Videos into Your Website, Blog, Social Networking Communities, and Mobile Campaigns

Using the <embed> code that is available with every video you upload to YouTube, you can easily copy, paste, and post your videos inside your website and your blog. The code can be customized in just a few clicks to size your videos and include a border, or not. You can also post your video links directly in Facebook status updates and tweets. Also, replacing the "www" in your video URL with an "m" will automatically generate a mobile version of your video that can be sent in group text messages.

11. Create an Annual "Thank You" Video

Donors and supporters always appreciate being thanked for their contribution, but traditionally most nonprofits express their gratitude via text in e-mails, blog posts, and website pages. A more visual, fresh approach is to create a video each year of staff members, volunteers, board members, and the communities that you serve expressing their thanks. It can be a simple 30-second video of 10 people saying "Thank You" (or holding up a "Thank You!" sign), or it can be more elaborate and longer, with interviews, text, and graphics. Again, a great place to feature this video is on your "Thanks for Your Donation" landing page.

GETTING STARTED WITH DIGITAL PHOTOGRAPHY

The last roll of Kodachrome film was developed at a small family-run business in Parsons, Kansas, on December 30, 2010. The rise of digital photography has brought to a close an important era in photography history, and at the same time has created unprecedented possibilities for nonprofits to use photos to capture their history and tell their stories. More than ever, nonprofits need to be building their digital photo libraries. Too often, nonprofits use the same small collection of photos over and over again in their print and Web campaigns, and while that may have worked in the past, your future success in utilizing social media and mobile technology is directly connected to your ability to create and share fresh, high-quality digital photos regularly.

Digital photography is not difficult to learn, and the responsibility is best delegated to your social media manager and communications staff, since they are the people who are most likely to be uploading the photos and sharing them on the Web. However, it's a responsibility that can also be shared with others at your nonprofit who have a passion for photography. Being confident behind a lens is crucial when capturing images at special events, fundraisers, conferences, protests, staff retreats, field visits, and other such occasions. Not everyone is comfortable walking up to individuals and groups of people and asking if she can take their photo. That's a skill that requires self-assurance and that can be learned only through experience. Whoever you decide should be the primary person for creating and managing the digital photography library at your organization, she must always have a digital camera on hand with charged batteries that can be grabbed at a moment's notice when the need arises.

To get started, you'll need to purchase a digital camera. A budget of $200 to $300 will get you a good-quality point-and-shoot pocket camera. Canon and Nikon brands are highly recommended. If your nonprofit foresees multiple digital photography campaigns in your future, you might want to invest $500 to $600 in a higher-quality hand-held camera. Good photo editing software will cost $100 or less. These are required investments for nonprofits that want to utilize social media and mobile technology. Without fresh digital images, your campaigns will be lackluster and will struggle to grab and maintain the attention of your supporters.

Finally, one of the most common questions nonprofits have about taking and publishing photos online is whether they need to use photo release forms. In general, the answer is no. If your nonprofit is publishing photos for information or educational purposes, and not for commercial use (that is, selling mugs, calendars, T-shirts, or other merchandise), then you do not need to secure a signed photo release form. However, for close-up shots of individuals that are to be used in interviews or feature stories, it doesn't hurt to get people's permission first. Privacy laws are blurry on this subject, and again, it's good to err on the side of caution. When you are photographing and publishing images of minors, always get a photo release from their parents. Still, thousands of nonprofits are creating and publishing slideshows of conferences, fundraisers, and volunteer events online every day. As with distributing video, use your best judgment and do only what you're comfortable with. For more information about legal issues and ethics pertaining to digital photography and copyright, see the National Press and Photographers Association's website at nppa.org.

INTRODUCTION TO FLICKR ACCOUNTS

Launched in 2004, Flickr is a photo-sharing website where nonprofits and other photography aficionados can organize and share their digital libraries. With an average of 20 million unique visitors a month, it is the largest photo-sharing community on the Web and hosts billions of photos from Flickr users all over the world. Most non-profits make their Flickr photos public so that they can be shared, but some nonprofits also have private Flickr accounts to serve as internal digital libraries that are accessible only to staff members and volunteers. Depending on your needs, you may want two Flickr accounts, one for public use and one for internal use. To create a Flickr account, go to flickr.com/signup, where you will first be prompted to create a Yahoo! account or log in to an account that you already have, since Flickr is owned by Yahoo!. Again, make sure that you are adding all new accounts and logins to your master login sheet.

ELEVEN FLICKR BEST PRACTICES FOR NONPROFITS

The core of a Flickr account is your "Photostream," which is a chronological display of your photos. You can then organize the photos from your photostream into "Collections" and "Sets." Flickr's tool set is multilayered, and it's very easy to overlook some of its best features. The best practices outlined here are for public, shareable Flickr accounts and ensure that your nonprofit is making the most of its Flickr account.

1. Upgrade to Flickr Pro

Sadly, most nonprofits don't invest in the $25 annual fee for Flickr Pro, with the result that they set up their Flickr account for mediocrity from the very start. Free Flickr accounts limit the number of sets you can create, do not offer collections or Flickr stats, and limit the number of photos you can upload to your account. To have good Flickr campaigns, you absolutely need the capability to create collections and an unlimited number of sets. Fortunately, a partnership between TechSoup.org and Flickr called Flickr for Good (flickr.com/good) allows nonprofits to apply for two Flickr Pro accounts per year for only $3 each.

2. Name All Photos

Flickr automatically names your photos as you upload them to your Flickr photostream. However, what your photos are named on your desktop is the name that Flickr associates with the photo in the photostream. Too many nonprofits out there are featuring photos on their Flickr account with names like DS10576 or July2011.jpg. Not good! Name photos properly as you upload them, or after uploading, you can simply click on the automated name and a field will appear where you can rename the photo. If your nonprofit does not have the time or capacity to name all photos, then delete the automated name and leave the name field blank. It's better to have photos with no name than named in gibberish.

3. Tag Your Best Photos

Flickr users search Flickr regularly for powerful and entertaining images. You don't need to tag every photo you upload, but at the very least, tag your best-quality photos and at least one from each set to optimize your Flickr SEO. Always include your nonprofit's name, city, and state as tags, as well as your country if you are outside the United States. Add cause tags that speak to your mission, such as hunger, homelessness, arts, international development, or animal welfare. Adding the tag "nonprofit" is a good idea, too.

4. Create Collections and Sets

Collections and sets can be created under "Organize & Create." It's a very simple "Create > Name > Drag and Drop" process. To begin, understand that collections hold sets. They should be used to organize multiple sets into larger general topics, such as events, programs, campaigns, or countries. For example, a nonprofit that hosts many events should create an "Events" collection, then drag and drop the set for each event into that collection. Another example is a nonprofit that offers multiple programs, such as a soup kitchen, a homeless shelter, and a job training program. Name a collection "Programs," then create additional sets for each program and place them in your new "Programs" collection. Additionally, many international development organizations use Flickr to tell their stories from the field by creating collections named after the countries in which they work. They then add sets of campaigns and events in that country to their "Zimbabwe" collection, for example. It's important that you map your organizational structure into collections and sets on Flickr early because you'll be integrating these collections and sets into your Web and social media campaigns often.

5. Format Collections and Sets

Absolutely add a two- or three-sentence description to each collection and set. A little-known trick is that you can use basic HTML in the descriptions, allowing links to your website, your blog, and your social networking communities. Since you will be posting your sets and collections throughout the Internet, take the extra five minutes and maximize your Flickr ROI by formatting all collections and sets.

6. Use HTML to Customize Your Profile and Reserve Your Flickr URL

Every Flickr account also has a Flickr Profile. Go to "Profile > Edit your profile information" and enter a one- or two-paragraph summary of your organization. You can use basic HTML to add bold, italics, and links to other websites. Also, go to "Profile > Edit your buddy icon" and upload your nonprofit's square avatar. Then, go to "Profile > Edit your screen name" and enter the full name of your organization. Finally, under "You > Your Account," you will find the option to reserve your Flickr URL, such as flickr.com/nonprofitorgs.

7. Add Contacts

Adding "Contacts" on Flickr is like sending friend requests on YouTube. Adding contacts is an easy way to announce your Flickr account to the Flickr community, and for each contact that you add, your avatar is then displayed on the new contact's profile, and vice versa. As with YouTube, take 10 minutes a week and add new contacts. Search for people in your area and for funders and other partner organizations. It's easy, and it makes a big impact on your Flickr brand and its potential for exponential exposure to the Flickr nonprofit community.

8. Join and Participate in Groups

There are tens of thousands of Flickr Groups. Do a quick search for groups that are in your area or are related to your mission and programs, and if they are active, then join those groups. You can then upload photos to those groups and participate in discussions that can help get your Flickr account increased exposure to the Flickr community. The groups that you are a member of are displayed on your profile page, so don't go overboard. You want to make sure that they are relevant to your nonprofit.

Over the years, many nonprofits have created their own groups, but with the exception of destination nonprofits, like museums (flickr.com/groups/brooklynmuseum), or nonprofits that host photo contests, like the Nature Conservancy (flickr.com/groups/thenature conservancy), it will be an uphill battle to get individuals to join your Flickr Group, much less upload photos to it and engage in discussions. Most nonprofits should put more focus on building their Flickr account and joining and participating in groups that are already created and active.

9. Promote Your Flickr Slideshows on Your Website and Blog, and in Your E-newsletter and Social Networking Communities

You can easily create Flickr slideshows of sets and your photostream by clicking the "Slideshow" link at the upper right. You can choose to show images and titles and set a slow, medium, or fast pace. Under the "Share" option, you can copy embed code that will enable you to insert the slideshow inside your website or blog. For e-newsletters, take a screenshot of your slideshow, then insert it into the body of your e-newsletter linking to the slideshow, such as flickr.com/nonprofitorgs/show. Additionally, post the link to the slideshow on Facebook and Twitter. That's when you'll really start to see your Flickr stats take off, and you'll probably get a few new contacts in the process.

10. Create Flickr Galleries That Speak to Your Organization's Mission and Programs

Flickr Galleries are a great way to feature and utilize some of the best photos uploaded to the Flickr community, and they can be easily created with just a few clicks. For example, if you are an environmental nonprofit, create an "Earth Gallery" with nature photos and landscapes. A wildlife conservation nonprofit could create a "Save the Tiger Gallery." Museums can curate Flickr Galleries of the best art from the Flickr community. Having a photo added to a gallery is the greatest expression of Flickr flattery, so take an hour or so and create three or four galleries. Users appreciate the acknowledgment, and again, it helps get your account more exposure in the wider Flickr community. Since galleries are limited in size to 18 photos, curating a Flickr Gallery requires only a minimal time investment.

11. Create an Annual "Thank You" Slideshow

Create an annual "Thank You" slideshow highlighting your achievements for the year. This should be like the YouTube "Thank You" video, and perhaps in place of it if you don't currently have the capacity to produce videos. Use photo titles and descriptions to add text to each photo. Then, of course, during the peak of your year-end online fundraising, promote the slideshow throughout your Web-based campaigns. People want to see progress and feel appreciated for their contribution to those achievements.

FINAL WORDS:
YOUTUBE AND FLICKR ARE NOT ENOUGH

The concept of sharing real-time video and digital photos becomes more mainstream with each passing day. Your social media and mobile communities often want to see videos recorded just minutes previously, or photos taken just seconds before, in tweets and status updates. Strategically speaking, your YouTube Channel and your Flickr account should serve as the online hubs to your nonprofit's best-produced video content and digital photos. Don't clutter your YouTube Channel or Flickr Photostream with low-resolution, off-the-cuff videos and photos taken from your smartphone or tablet. It's best to use Twitter or yfrog for your real-time mobile campaigns. That said, smartphones and tablets will probably evolve to include higher-quality video recorders and digital cameras in the next few years, possibly rendering pocket camcorders and digital cameras obsolete. Even if this happens, it's still best to keep your desktop and mobile video and digital photo campaigns separate because the two require different tool sets and approaches. Telling and sharing your nonprofit's stories through video and digital photography after they have occurred is quite different from telling the story while it's happening.

Nonprofit Examples of Excellence: YouTube

- Anaheim Ballet: youtube.com/anaheimballet

- Best Friends Animal Society: youtube.com/bestfriendsvideos

- Big Cat Rescue: youtube.com/bigcatrescue

- Greenpeace International: youtube.com/greenpeacevideo

- Ocean Conservancy: youtube.com/oceanconservancy

Nonprofit Examples of Excellence: Flickr

- 350.org: flickr.com/350org

- American Red Cross: flickr.com/americanredcross

- Asia Society: flickr.com/asiasociety

- San Francisco Museum of Modern Art: flickr.com/sfmoma

- U.N. Refugee Agency: flickr.com/unhcr

Google This!

- ❏ Youtube.com/nonprofitorgs

- ❏ Youtube nonprofit cosmic panda

- ❏ Youtube.com/nonprofitvideoawards

- ❏ Youtube-global.blogspot.com

- ❏ Animoto for a cause

- ❏ Techsoup digital storytelling challenge

- ❏ Top 10 reviews pocket camcorders

- ❏ Pocket camcorder tripod

- ❏ Pocket camcorder wide-angle lens

- ❏ Pocket camcorder video light

- ❏ Top 10 reviews video editing software

- ❏ Top 10 reviews compact digital cameras

- ❏ Top 10 reviews photo editing software

- ❑ Photo and video release form
- ❑ Youtube thank you from smile train
- ❑ Flickr.com/upgrade
- ❑ Flickr.com/nonprofitorgs
- ❑ Flickr.com/good
- ❑ Flickr.com/creativecommons

6

LINKEDIN

Hands-down, LinkedIn is one of the best tools for galvanizing and organizing supporters, especially volunteers. LinkedIn Groups in particular give them a means to network virtually and come together offline. Oftentimes, LinkedIn isn't a first choice when an organization is considering its social media strategies, but my advice is to not skip this one—it's on a par with the likes of Twitter and Facebook!

—*Dupe O. Ajayi, external affairs manager,*
Taproot Foundation

THE BIG PICTURE: MERGING YOUR PERSONAL AND PROFESSIONAL BRANDS

LinkedIn is a social networking website for professionals. Launched in 2003, LinkedIn has grown steadily in traffic and users year after year, and as a result, it now has more than 100 million users in more than 200 countries. Unlike on Facebook, very little personal information is shared on LinkedIn. The tool set was built primarily to make professional connections and build an online résumé. For the benefit of her nonprofit and her career, every nonprofit professional should have a presence on LinkedIn.

The first step is to sign up and build your personal profile, then "Connect" with past and present work colleagues, classmates, and friends. From there, you can then join "Groups" (or create your own), engage in "Answers," and claim and set up your "Company Page" to promote your nonprofit. It's very important to understand that on LinkedIn, there is no separation of the personal and the professional. You use your personal profile both to build your personal brand and to promote your nonprofit to the LinkedIn community. Your personal identity and your nonprofit brand are inextricably combined inside the LinkedIn community.

Some nonprofit professionals are uncomfortable merging their personal and professional identities online, especially on Facebook. Sharing personal photos and status updates with friends, family members, donors, clients, and coworkers can make for an awkward Facebook experience. That's why LinkedIn is an excellent alternative for those who hesitate to personally social network with colleagues for privacy reasons. Yes, your identities are merged on LinkedIn, but there's no photo functionality, gaming, or personal quizzes. LinkedIn is all professional; it's even a little stiff in comparison to Facebook, but the two have entirely different purposes. That said, many nonprofit professionals don't think twice about merging their personal and professional lives online. For those who do, separating real friends on Facebook from your professional connections on LinkedIn allows you to embrace both personal and professional social networking comfortably.

INTRODUCTION TO LINKEDIN PROFILES

A LinkedIn Profile primarily serves as an online résumé that summarizes your work experience, education, skills, and professional awards and accolades. As social networking components are built in, you can then send requests to connect, import your blog or news feed, and send out "Updates" to your connections. The LinkedIn community and tool set are vast. There's much to explore and experiment with. You should plan on allocating at least one hour a week to building your personal brand recognition inside of LinkedIn and nurturing connections. Again, the line between personal and professional is blurry on LinkedIn, so much so that it's completely respectable to use LinkedIn for personal reasons during office hours.

ELEVEN PROFILE TIPS FOR NONPROFIT PROFESSIONALS

Unless you plan on working at your current nonprofit for the rest of your life, it's entirely possible that during your next job search, recruiters and your future boss will be browsing your LinkedIn Profile. In fact, as long as you follow the tips outlined here, you'll probably want to add your LinkedIn Profile vanity URL to your résumé. Until then, when you're advocating for the nonprofit where you currently work, the professionalism of your profile directly reflects upon your nonprofit. Though it may take four to five hours, you should make the effort and invest the time necessary to complete your LinkedIn Profile in order to maximize its full potential. To create and then set up a profile on LinkedIn, go to linkedin.com/reg/join, then go to "Profile > Edit Profile" and follow the tips given here. You'll also want to click on your name in the upper right of LinkedIn and select "Settings" to configure your privacy settings and e-mail notifications.

1. Fill Out Your Profile to "100 Percent Completeness"

As you set up your profile, LinkedIn will display a thermometer indicating the percent to which your profile is complete. Fill out all fields until you reach 100 percent. You should add a brief, succinct bio to the summary field. Include the majority of your work experience and all schools you attended (even study abroad programs). Maximize the website and Twitter fields. Fill out interests, groups and associations, and honors and awards. There are also special sections of your profile where you can list certifications, languages, patents, skills, and publications. For security reasons, do not add your phone number or mailing address. Connections can contact you directly through LinkedIn Mail. A profile that is 100 percent completed makes a strong first impression upon LinkedIn members and anyone who might be searching for you in Google, Bing, or Yahoo!. LinkedIn Profiles rank very high in search results, so make sure yours is filled to 100 percent completeness.

2. Use a Professional Photo for Your Profile Photo

It's best to use a profile photo on LinkedIn that speaks to your professional career, not your personal life (that is, not photos that were taken on vacation, with the family, in costume, and so on). Some personality is OK, but if you wouldn't use a photo on the "Staff" page of your nonprofit's website, then don't use it on LinkedIn, either. In the spirit of merging the personal with the professional, you can help build your nonprofit's brand recognition in the LinkedIn community by adding your nonprofit's Twibbon to your profile picture. Also, it's worth noting that your profile cannot reach 100 percent completeness without your uploading a photo. The LinkedIn community is skeptical of profiles without photos, thinking that they may be spammers, so LinkedIn makes uploading a photo a requirement for completion.

3. Customize Your Headline

By default, LinkedIn uses the title of your current position as your "Professional Headline." You can customize your headline and add more detail and personality by going to "Edit Profile." When people browse connections on LinkedIn, it's your headline that is displayed most prominently, so craft it to make a strong first impression and summarize your most valuable skills.

4. Reserve Your LinkedIn Public Profile Vanity URL

To make it easier for you to promote your LinkedIn Profile online, in e-mail, and on your résumé, it's crucial that you go to "Edit Profile > Edit Public Profile >" and set your public profile URL. Use your first and last names to optimize search engine results, such as linkedin.com/in/heathermansfield. Fortunately, you can change your vanity URL at a later date if necessary—if you get married and change your name, for example.

5. Make Connections

Once you have set up your profile, you are ready to go public. Go to "People" and search individually by name, or import your contacts from your e-mail address books. You can also search for past work colleagues by going to "Companies" and searching for the company pages of places where you used to work (these are also accessible on the public view of your profile by clicking the company page icon next to each of your past employers' names). When you find people you know, go to their profile and add them to your network. Finally, you should add your LinkedIn Profile vanity URL to your work e-mail signature.

6. Give Recommendations

Featured on your profile, "Recommendations" are like references, and they are highly prized and much sought after on LinkedIn. Connections can write a paragraph or two about working with you and about your skill set and professional attributes, and vice versa. Recommendations are, of course, meant to be positive. To get recommendations, however, in most cases you have to give recommendations. Make a commitment to give one or two a month. Proper etiquette is to reciprocate with anyone who gives you a recommendation (although not everyone does so). Don't take it too personally if you don't get one in return. More than likely, the person is just busy or not that active on LinkedIn. Still, hopefully, within a year you'll have five or more recommendations.

7. Post Authentic Updates—Don't Sync with Twitter!

Featured on the "Home" view of LinkedIn are the updates that have been posted by your connections. What you usually see there (and what most people ignore) are tweets that have been automatically posted in the LinkedIn news feed from your personal profile. Resist the urge and do not automate! Automated tweets just clutter the feed, and many people find them annoying. Make an effort to post authentic updates at least once a week. You're more likely to get noticed and receive comments and likes as well when you post authentically. It's worth noting that your most recent update is always featured at the top of your profile, so post updates strategically.

8. Use LinkedIn Applications

LinkedIn has a small application directory that allows you to feature your blog and PowerPoint presentations directly on your profile, among other things. To browse available applications, go to "Edit Profile > Add an application" and add at least one application. They add some color and pizzazz that can easily grab the attention of people who visit your profile.

9. Join, Participate in, and Display LinkedIn Groups on Your Profile

There are tens of thousands of groups on LinkedIn on topics ranging from "Autism Speaks" to "Zoo and Aquarium Professionals." There are also a wide variety of groups related to nonprofit professional networking, job seeking, fundraising, communications, and philanthropy. You should browse and join groups that are related to your nonprofit's mission and programs, along with those that are specialized for the nonprofit sector, and then post links to your blog or website in discussions or promotions and engage fellow members. Be sure to monitor your LinkedIn referring traffic to your website and blog. The click-through rate on LinkedIn is phenomenal, often higher than that for Twitter or Facebook, provided your content is good. You'll also probably start receiving more requests to connect, and possibly a recommendation or two, if you are active in groups. It's beneficial to both your personal and nonprofit brands for you to spend a couple of hours per month participating in groups. Finally, be sure to allow your groups (under settings) to be featured on your profile. The groups you join and display on your LinkedIn Profile say a lot about who you are and where your interests lie.

10. Experiment with Answers

If you enjoy chatting online with strangers, then it's worth experimenting with LinkedIn Answers. There is a nonprofit category where you can ask or answer questions in subcategories related to nonprofit fundraising, nonprofit management, philanthropy, and social entrepreneurship. The more you participate, the higher you move up the "Top Experts" list. At a minimum, participate once or twice a month to get your name out on LinkedIn.

11. Don't Engage the Narcissists!

There are countless experts, masters, mavens, rock stars, and gurus on LinkedIn. The vast majority are respectful, courteous, and helpful, but some are over the top in their arrogance and expertise. People in the nonprofit sector in general are humble and very good at keeping their egos in check, but occasionally you will encounter an outrageous personality on LinkedIn who enjoys inciting arguments with people, claiming absolutes, and constantly spamming your group. Experience will teach you that it's best to just ignore or block these people. The more you engage them, the worse it gets. Encountering such narcissists is rare, but it is a uniquely LinkedIn experience that can be shocking to some nonprofit professionals when they first encounter it.

INTRODUCTION TO LINKEDIN GROUPS

LinkedIn Groups function as subcommunities for professional networking and expertise swapping inside the greater LinkedIn community, and they can be a powerhouse in terms of return on investment (ROI) when they are utilized and engaged effectively. Tragically, most nonprofits have yet to tap into the power of LinkedIn Groups. Over the years, many have tried to create their own groups, but with only limited knowledge of the group tool set, they were unlikely to experience much success, and thus they abandoned their group too soon. Those that have stuck it out and invested time in their group are just now starting to reap the benefits.

To create a LinkedIn Group for your nonprofit, go to "Groups > Create Group." The hardest decision you'll have to make is deciding what to name your group. Many nonprofits, of course, name their group after their nonprofit, but unless you are a nonprofit that offers professional or volunteer services, you may have a hard time building interest in your group if you do so. For example, people on LinkedIn may be more interested in joining a group called "Sustainable Fishing" than a group called "Marine Conservation Biology Institute," or a group called "Cancer Survivors Network" rather than one called "American Cancer Society." The reason many nonprofit LinkedIn Groups have grown stagnant is that their name narrows the scope of conversation and doesn't appeal to potential new members. People are interested in discussing sustainable fishing and surviving cancer, but not necessarily in discussing the Marine Conservation Biology Institute or the American Cancer Society.

The good news is that you can change your group name up to four times. Experiment with the name of your group and settle on the name that results in the most new members. It's much better to have a large group that is not named after your nonprofit than a small group with your nonprofit's name. Eventually, if your group grows to 20,000 or 30,000, you can then change the name to that of your nonprofit to maximize your nonprofit's brand inside the LinkedIn community, but to begin, you may need to be more creative by launching a cause-based LinkedIn Group.

ELEVEN LINKEDIN GROUP MANAGEMENT BEST PRACTICES FOR NONPROFITS

There are many perks to being the manager of a successful LinkedIn Group, and it is worth the effort to grow and nurture your group. To jump-start your group, you will need to promote it on your website, in your e-newsletter, and to your social networking communities. You can also easily invite all your connections on LinkedIn to join—a tip that should be shared with other staff members and volunteers. As with most other communities, the magic number when you no longer need to actively promote your group and it grows on its own hovers around the 5,000-member benchmark. When your group reaches that size, it's likely to produce more traffic to your website and new e-newsletter subscribers than 10,000 fans on Facebook or followers on Twitter will do. In the era of social media, LinkedIn Groups have been one of the most underutilized and overlooked tools available to nonprofits.

1. Require Approval to Join

The reason to require approval is that if you have to log in regularly to approve pending new members, this gives you, as "Group Manager," a better sense of how quickly (or not) your group is growing. By default, logging in regularly to approve new members also makes you a better group manager, because while you are logged in, you should also be participating in discussions and managing spam. In the past, most nonprofits have set up groups without requiring approval or made their group an open group, thinking that this is an easy way to have a presence on LinkedIn without having to invest a lot of time. It doesn't work, however. If your group is overrun by spammers for a month or more, or if discussions go silent, then your group loses all credibility and members will begin to leave en masse. Requiring approval to join forces you to be engaged in your group on a regular basis and take responsibility for monitoring spam. The primary reason that nonprofit LinkedIn Groups have not done well is that they have been poorly managed. Finally, keeping your group closed will pique the curiosity of potential new members and increase the likelihood that they will join. If they can see your group content without joining and it has been a slow week or two in freshly posted content or you haven't had a chance yet to delete recent spam, then you have likely lost them as a member of your group.

2. Keep Your Group's Summary and Description Brief

Limit your LinkedIn "Group Summary" and "Group Description" to one paragraph each that clarifies some possible topics of discussion for your group. Many nonprofits use their mission statement, thus limiting the growth of their group. Again, people don't want to join groups to talk about your nonprofit. They want to join groups to talk about issues and ideas. If you do name your group after your nonprofit, then clearly specify in the group summary and group description that people are encouraged to discuss issues and ideas (list a broad range of possible topics to lure them in). If you name your group after a cause, then add a sentence at the end of your group summary and group description that says, "This group was created and is managed by [Nonprofit Name]."

You're also given the opportunity to add a website link to your group home page. Use your nonprofit's website. Don't try to be clever and put your Facebook Page or Twitter Profile. People see right through that and ignore it more often than not. You're attempting to build a community on LinkedIn, not to build your Facebook or Twitter community. Subtlety is an art on the Social Web. Finally, you can use the same paragraph for your group summary and group description. The group description is meant to be longer, but that's not necessary if you craft a powerful, succinct one-paragraph blurb about your group and its purpose.

3. Use a Horizontal Avatar

LinkedIn Groups are the only type of community discussed in this book that uses a rectangular avatar instead of a square one. If you name your group after your nonprofit, then your horizontal logo is fine for your LinkedIn Group's avatar. If not, you'll need to enlist a designer who can create one, or you can use a photo. Keep in mind that your avatar will probably be displayed on hundreds, and hopefully thousands, of LinkedIn Profiles and featured in search results and the news feeds of your new members when they join your group. It needs to be a strong avatar that makes a solid first impression.

4. Enable Promotions and Jobs

Discussions are meant for discussion, not for promoting events, Webinars, or services that are available to the nonprofit sector. To help you keep overzealous marketers from spamming your LinkedIn discussions, enable the "Promotions" function. You can easily move an inappropriately posted discussion to promotions by simply flagging the discussion post. This will keep your discussions clutter-free. You should also enable the "Jobs" function to empower LinkedIn members to share and post jobs. You never know. You could help one of your members find his dream job.

5. Publish Group Rules

You must post clear "Group Rules." The best practice is to ask that members post all promotional content under promotions and jobs, and that discussions be reserved solely for sharing resources, discussing issues and ideas, and seeking advice. As your group grows larger, it's a mathematical certainty that you will get more spam from marketers. Some of these marketers will not realize that they are spamming and will get angry when you delete their content, so having group rules gives the group manager the power to delete or recategorize with conviction. The ability to post group rules is under "Manage > Group Rules." Once the rules are posted, they are then featured in the upper right of your group's home page.

6. Maximize the Group Templates Feature

LinkedIn Group templates are the biggest perk of managing a LinkedIn Group, and yet the vast majority of nonprofits do not utilize them! Under "Manage > Templates," you can create a "Request-to-Join" message and a "Welcome" message; these are e-mailed to pending new members when they request to join, and to approved new members after you approve them. Definitely utilize the templates feature to your nonprofit's advantage by creating a request-to-join template that thanks potential members for their interest and lets them know that they will be approved shortly, and that in the meantime they can visit your website, like you on Facebook, or follow you on Twitter. Then, for the welcome template, welcome them to your group, list your group rules, let them know you are looking forward to their participation, and then, of course, mention your website and social networking communities. Be tactful and err on the side of subtlety, but templates are high in ROI and are your payoff for taking the time necessary to create, promote, and manage a LinkedIn Group.

7. Don't Use News Feeds

You can add your nonprofit's news or blog feed to your group, but it's best to resist the temptation. Instead, post news and new blog posts manually. The news feed function posts content with a generic "RSS" avatar (rather than your personal avatar) and lacks personality. Most people ignore automated posts on LinkedIn, and on most other communities as well.

8. Block and Delete Spammers

To be a successful LinkedIn Group manager, you are going to have to develop a bit of a thick skin. Sometimes you have to be tough and delete content, or even block people from being members. This is rare, but it is guaranteed to happen. A lot of marketers will join your group simply to post their content so that they reach new customers and increase their website or blog traffic. They have no intention of ever participating in discussions. Some of the content they post is obviously spam, such as "Earn $200 a day working from home!" and you can delete it and block the member from your group without a second thought. These people know they are spamming. Other content is sometimes gray in its spam factor; for example, someone may be selling business cards or her upcoming Webinar on how businesses can use social media. These people will tell you that their product is great for the nonprofit sector too, and while that may be true, there are thousands of business networking groups on LinkedIn. If you let one in, then more and more will follow. Do yourself, your members, and LinkedIn a favor and get rid of the clutter. Allow only content that directly relates to your group summary and group description. It will make your group more productive and your ROI much higher.

9. Post and Participate in Your Own Discussions

In the beginning, you will need to jump-start your LinkedIn Group's content. Never launch a group without posting discussions, and if no one posts a discussion in four or five days, then post your own. A lull in activity is glaringly obvious. When people join your group, they are given the option of receiving daily or weekly e-mail updates of group activity. The e-mail updates feature recent discussions and jobs (not promotions), and if there is no activity, then no e-mail updates are sent out. These e-mails produce high click-through rates, especially for those discussions selected as "Manager's Choice," so make sure there is always fresh content and that you rotate your manager's choice discussions at least twice a month. It's also worth noting that if you don't monitor spam and delete it quickly, it will get e-mailed to your group as well. That's why you should never abandon your LinkedIn Group!

10. Send Monthly Announcements

Another perk that is high in ROI is the ability to send "Announcements" to your group members. LinkedIn allows you to send one a week, but less often is better. People pay much more attention and are less likely to classify your announcements as spammish if you send them only once a month. A good idea is to feature the top three discussions of the month in an announcement, and then at the end add a subtle pitch for your nonprofit. Plan your announcements strategically. They outperform a tweet or a Facebook status update any day of the week, so you know that when you send one out, people are listening.

11. Create Subgroups when You Reach 5,000 Members

You should not create "Subgroups" until your primary group reaches 5,000 members. Creating subgroups too early will fragment your community and confuse members regarding where they should invest their time in discussions. When you do reach 5,000, launch one subgroup, then send out an announcement and add a "New Subgroup!" pitch to your templates. Give the subgroup time to grow and flourish, and then perhaps launch another. You have to be disciplined and strategic to create subgroups that interest and engage members. You can create a subgroup under "Manage > Create a Subgroup."

CLAIMING YOUR NONPROFIT'S LINKEDIN COMPANY PAGE

Odds are that your nonprofit has a "Company Page" on LinkedIn. If you or any of your past employees, interns, or hired consultants or contractors has a personal profile on LinkedIn and has added her position at your nonprofit to her work experience, then by default she has created a company page for your nonprofit. The easiest way to locate the page is to go to your personal profile and click on the company page icon next to your nonprofit's name. If you don't have a LinkedIn Profile yet, a quick search for your nonprofit's name in "Companies" will reveal whether you have a page or not.

LinkedIn Company Pages were launched in 2008, but it wasn't until 2010 that nonprofits and businesses could "Claim" their page. Initially, all you could do was upload a logo, add a description and website link, select company "Specialties" and "Industry," and insert an RSS/news feed. Then in April 2010, LinkedIn members could begin "Following" company pages to view company activity (new jobs, hires, and so on) in their LinkedIn news feed. Next, in November 2010, LinkedIn launched the ability to post "Services" and view "Analytics," allowing you to add detailed descriptions of your non-profit's services with photos and website links and monitor daily traffic to your company page.

To claim your nonprofit's company page, go to "Companies > Add a Company," and then search for your nonprofit by name. Once you have found your nonprofit's company page, or you're prompted to create a new one because your nonprofit does not yet have one, you must then enter a work e-mail address to claim the page. LinkedIn will not accept Gmail, Yahoo!, Hotmail, and other such e-mail addresses. Then you'll be asked to verify the e-mail address in an e-mail from LinkedIn; once you've verified it, you can then upload your logo, a short description of your nonprofit, a website link, your blog, and Twitter feeds and embed YouTube videos. If you are a service organization, add the services you offer (counseling, low-income housing, career training, and so on). Finally, once you have set up your company page, be sure to incorporate a follow request into your group templates and let your fans, followers, and friends on social networking sites know about your new company page. All signs point to LinkedIn continuing to build the functionality of company pages, and it's likely that they will become an integral part of the LinkedIn community, so the sooner your nonprofit gets invested in building and promoting your company page, the better.

FINAL WORDS:
SLOW AND STEADY IS SMART
IN SOCIAL MEDIA

LinkedIn was pioneering social networking and Web 2.0 before the idea of Facebook had even been born. It is a shining example of the power of early adoption and forward thinking balanced with the wisdom of going slowly and steadily. It took its time rolling out new features and tools that were well built and useful. It didn't expect overnight success or sacrifice quality to get it. As a result, it is today the largest professional social networking site on the Web. It is the modern Aesop's Fable of slow and steady winning the race.

In terms of strategy, slow and steady in social media is smart, and your nonprofit would be wise to embrace it. Do not expect overnight success or immediate results. Initially your communities will grow slowly, but once that Facebook Page, LinkedIn Group, or Twitter Profile hits 5,000, then the power of exponential growth will begin to kick in. It is worth the time investment and the wait, but if you're impatient and demanding and give up too soon or launch mediocre campaigns, then the race is yours to lose.

Nonprofit Examples of Excellence: LinkedIn Groups

- Anita Borg Institute for Women and Technology

- BoardSource

- Global Fund for Women

- Habitat for Humanity

- Idealist.org

Google This!

- ❏ Learn.linkedin.com

- ❏ Social media for nonprofit organizations linkedin group

- ❏ Mobile technology for nonprofit organizations linkedin group

- ❏ Linkedin.com/company/taprootfoundation

BLOGGING

Our blog is the hub of our organization's social media strategy. It provides us an easy way to tell our stories on Facebook and Twitter, and because our blog posts are more personal than press releases and Web page text, it really allows people to get a sense of who we are as people, and not just who we are as an organization.

—Allison Palmer, director of digital
initiatives, GLAAD (Gay & Lesbian
Alliance Against Defamation)

THE BIG PICTURE: CREATING AND DISTRIBUTING CONTENT FOR THE SOCIAL WEB

The Social Web is driven by fresh content. Old news just doesn't get retweeted or liked. To maximize your nonprofit's exposure on social media sites, you need to be creating fresh content on a consistent basis. Some nonprofits do that by regularly posting news articles on their website, but posting that same content in a blog format, where supporters can comment, interact, and easily share your blog posts with their own communities, is increasingly becoming a more powerful strategy. If a blog is designed and written well, it can transform your nonprofit's online brand recognition. In fact, for many nonprofits that are struggling to build their e-newsletter lists, online donations, and social networking communities, blogging is often the missing piece in their online communications and development strategies—they just don't know it (yet).

Nonprofits that do not blog, or that don't get much traction on their blog, still think of blogging like it's 2005. Back then, the best practice was to use blogging to write long editorial pieces, usually by the executive director, to "add a human voice" to their organization. Well, today, there's no shortage of tools available that enable your nonprofit to "be human," and the patience to read long editorial pieces is waning with each passing tweet, text, status update, and check-in. Many nonprofits also don't consider blogging because of another outdated myth—that they need to blog every day. For many nonprofits, that's an overwhelming, time-consuming commitment that immediately invokes fears of writer's block and inefficient use of staff time. In reality, you don't need to blog every day. Once or twice a week is just fine.

With almost 200 million blogs worldwide generating nearly 1 million blog posts daily, many nonprofits may think that the world does not need another blogger—that there's no space left in the blogosphere for your nonprofit—but that's simply not the case. There's always room for a well-designed, well-written blog. The truth is that blogging is easier and much more fun than it was just five short years ago. It's also more vital to the overall success of your nonprofit's online campaigns than it has ever been. Here are six reasons why:

- *Blogging allows your nonprofit to have a consistent stream of fresh, timely new content to tweet, share on Facebook, use in your e-newsletter, and so on.* Blogging allows nonprofits to easily publish and distribute content that's timely and relevant to the here and now. Through blogging, nonprofits can tell their stories, break news, comment on breaking news, and share resources quickly with their supporters in social networking communities, who then in turn often share this information with their own communities. Again, old news just doesn't garner a response on social networking sites. Social networking communities are heavily influenced by and responsive to the 24/7 news cycle. Blogging allows your nonprofit to tap into that cycle directly. The same is true of e-newsletters. Readers are much more likely to open an e-mail if it is connected to current news or recent internal developments at your nonprofit.

- *Blogging improves your search engine results.* In recent years, search engines like Google and Yahoo! have dramatically changed the way they archive the Web and list Web pages in their search results. Over the last decade, search engine optimization (SEO) spammers became so aggressive in their use of keyword meta tags to manipulate search engine results that Google, Yahoo!, and others have now changed their search "spiders" to prioritize keywords in page titles over keyword meta tags. There's also the fact that these spiders love new, fresh content (especially from blogs), and every new blog post you publish to the Web helps get their attention. With some focus and strategic titling of your blog posts, your blog could appear on page one of search engine results within a few months.

- *Blogging helps you build your e-newsletter and group text messaging lists.* People are much more likely to sign up for your e-newsletter and group text messaging campaigns from your blog than from your website. The personal nature of blogging can often pique a reader's interest much more than the static content on your website and thus inspire her to get more involved, that is, to subscribe to your e-newsletter and your group text messaging campaigns.

- *Blogging allows you to grow the number of fans and followers you have on social networking sites.* Similarly, potential friends, followers, and fans are much more likely to join your social networking communities from your blog than from your website. Once your blog starts to get some momentum, you will also notice a faster growth of new friends, followers, and fans.

- *Blogging can empower your mobile website.* A blog can serve as the primary content source for your mobile website. Using RSS, blogging allows your nonprofit to launch a mobile website with minimal effort and expense.

- *Blogging gives you access to valuable statistics and data.* Blogging platforms provide your nonprofit with valuable stats and data, including referring websites, the links clicked in your blog posts, how much traffic each post receives, and daily, weekly, and monthly stats reports. They also provide the keywords searched in search engines that resulted in traffic to your blog. The information also helps reveal what social networking communities are most valuable in terms of click-through rates and what keywords you should be using in blog titles.

SELECTING A BLOGGING PLATFORM

Most professional bloggers choose WordPress as their blogging platform, and for very good reasons. It's a phenomenal tool that is highly favored by search engines. It's free, well built, and consistently praised and adored by the blogosphere. It makes an excellent choice for nonprofits. That said, some new blogging platforms have been launched in recent years that some of the early adopters in the nonprofit sector have embraced and recommended for this book. Again, WordPress is an excellent choice, but you should also conduct some research into the other platforms before making your final decision.

- *WordPress.org.* WordPress.org is a blogging platform that also doubles as a content management system (CMS) for many nonprofit websites. It's free to download and must be hosted on a server. It is completely customizable; there are thousands of WordPress themes and plug-ins available to download to design and add functionality to your blog. You can also embed a WordPress.org blog inside your nonprofit's website with a little help from your website designer.

- *WordPress.com.* WordPress.com is a free blogging platform that does not require third-party hosting. Instead, the blog is hosted inside of WordPress.com. Its theme choice is limited and you cannot add plug-ins, but it's powerful, extremely easy to use, and customizable enough to allow a design that matches the professionalism of your other online branding. It provides a dashboard of useful stats and a suite of built-in widgets that match the needs of most nonprofits. WordPress.com is an excellent option for those nonprofits that do not have the capacity or tech know-how necessary to set up a WordPress.org blog.

- *TypePad.* TypePad is another well-respected blogging platform that is often used by professional bloggers. Although it is not free (it costs $15 to $30 per month), TypePad is a fully customizable blogging platform that offers hundreds of themes to choose from as a starting point for your design, a suite of widgets, traffic stats, and a community feature that allows supporters to "Follow" your blog. It also offers its customers support and free Webinars.

- *Squarespace.* Although Squarespace (2004) has been around almost as long as WordPress (2003), it has only recently begun to receive buzz in the nonprofit sector. It was originally launched as a do-it-yourself website platform, but in recent years it has evolved to add blogging and social media components. You can use it as a CMS for your website, for your blog, or for both. One of its advantages is that it makes it very easy to have a website and a blog hosted under the same domain name. Although the number of themes it offers is limited compared to those offered by WordPress and TypePad, its themes are hip, modern, and very Web 2.0—and completely customizable. Its monthly fees range from $12 to $36.

- *Tumblr.* Launched in 2007, Tumblr is part blogging platform, part social networking community, and part social media dashboard. Although it's not ideal for your nonprofit's primary blog, Tumblr makes an interesting choice for secondary blogs that are specific to a campaign or issue. Tumblr is cutting-edge blogging and is likely to do some interesting integration with mobile technology in coming years. It's free, so it wouldn't hurt to sign up and register your username, such as doctorswithoutborders.tumblr.com.

ELEVEN BLOG DESIGN BEST PRACTICES FOR NONPROFITS

Making a strong first impression on your readers is critical to the success of your nonprofit's blog. Your blog's return on investment (ROI) is directly related to its design and its integration of social media. Readers will not take your blog content seriously if your blog looks as if it was set up and is maintained by an amateur. Your blog should have the highest in design and implementation standards. The blogosphere today is powerful and highly professional. It's better not to blog than to blog poorly. Your blog can have excellent content, but if the first impression that it gives is poor, most people won't bother reading it.

1. Use a Simple Design That Allows a Custom Header

Like your website, your blog should be designed in Web 2.0 style. It needs to be simple, visually powerful, and spacious. A two-column layout consisting of a blog post column on the left and a promotional column (usually three inches or less) on the right where you feature pitches and widgets is best. Too much clutter and multiple columns can easily overwhelm and distract readers. A two-column layout also decreases the need to scroll while reading because the blog post column is usually wider than with a three-column layout. All blog posts should be published on a white background with black text, then choose one color from your nonprofit's branding to highlight links.

Most important, your blog should have a header across the top that matches your nonprofit's overall branding. If you have to hire a professional designer to create a banner for your blog, then do it. It is a required expense. Quite often you can also use this banner on your website and your e-newsletter, so it's a value-added investment. Do not underestimate the importance of this banner! Readers simply will not take your blog seriously if it is poorly designed.

Finally, when setting up your blog, you will be prompted to name your blog. The name will be displayed on every page title and will affect your blog's SEO, so it's a good idea to consider naming your blog something more creative and strategic than [Your Nonprofit's Name]'s Blog, such as "Cool Green Science: The Conservation Blog of the Nature Conservancy" or "The ASPCA Blog: Talk Action, Take Action." That said, for SEO reasons, make sure that your nonprofit's name and the word *blog* are included in the title.

2. Use Your Avatar as Your Blog Picture

Your nonprofit's avatar should be used for your blog picture. This image is displayed when you post responses to comments or participate in other blogs. If your blog is written by a specific personality (or multiple people), another option is to use her image with a Twibbon of your nonprofit's avatar in the lower right of her personal image.

Again, the use of your avatar needs to be consistent and present across all social media platforms and communities.

3. Feature the Ability to Subscribe to Your E-newsletter and Text Campaigns and to Join Your Social Networking Communities

As on your website, the upper right-hand corner of your promotional column is the most valuable section of your blog in terms of ROI. There you should feature the ability to subscribe to your e-newsletter, your text campaigns, and your blog via RSS, and add the social networking icons for your Facebook Page, Twitter Profile, YouTube Channel, Flickr account, and so on. As your blog traffic increases, you'll begin to notice a significant increase in new subscribers, friends, followers, and fans. You'll need to use a HTML/text widget to add your subscribe information and icons to your blog. It's tragic how many nonprofits do not do this simply because they do not know basic HTML.

4. Limit Your Use of Third-Party Widgets

There's no shortage of third-party widgets available to embed in your blog, but more often than not, they just make your blog look messy and unprofessional. Use them sparingly! Unless they can be formatted to be the same size and be consistent in their use of color, avoid using widgets on your blog. They were cool in 2007, but not anymore.

5. Invest Time and Effort in Crafting Your Pages

Pages are different from blog posts. Like secondary pages featured in the primary navigation on your website, blog pages are featured in the primary navigation on your blog and are visible on every blog post you publish. Take your time crafting the content for these pages, and use them to feature your most important campaigns and pitches. Ideas for pages include such things as "About Us," "Our Work," "Events," "Get Involved," "Take Action," and "Donate." The content for these pages can be more static in nature. As a general rule, keep them limited to two or three paragraphs, with at least one link to your website worked into the content on every page. Finally, each page should include a photo. It's best if the photos on every page are the same size.

6. Allow Comments, but Moderate Them

It's hard to take a blog that doesn't allow comments seriously. Some nonprofits are fearful of rogue comments and thus disable them, but that's silly. For most nonprofits, rogue comments are rare. Spam comments are likely to be more of an issue for nonprofits than rude, disrespectful comments. Even if you're a nonprofit that works on controversial issues, you should still allow comments. You don't have to approve all of them. All blogging platforms have a notification system that allows you to moderate (approve or disapprove) comments before they go live. To have a blog without comment functionality is like having a Facebook Page with no wall. It just doesn't work.

7. Add Share Functionality

Depending upon the blog platform you're using, your blog may automatically come with share functionality, or you may have to add a plug-in, manually embed the code for Twitter and Facebook buttons, or use a service like ShareThis (sharethis.com) or AddThis (addthis.com). Unfortunately, the ease of making blog posts shareable varies widely among blogging platforms. Whether the blog platform makes sharing easy should weigh heavily in your decision of what platform to use.

8. Add Search Functionality

More often than not, adding a "Search" box to a blog is as simple as checking a box or dragging and dropping a built-in widget. Readers search often, so be sure to feature your search function higher in your promotional column.

9. Feature Recent Posts and Recent Comments

Featuring recent posts and recent comments in your promotional column prolongs the period in which past posts can get traffic and comments. Adding this functionality is usually as simple as dragging and dropping built-in widgets or adding a plug-in. Depending on space, you should feature five to ten recent posts and comments somewhere near the middle of your promotional column.

10. Use Photos and/or Video in All Blog Posts

As a general rule, you should have at least one photo at the upper right of every blog post because blog posts with images tend to get more traction. Try to be consistent in your use of photos in all blog posts: 300 pixels by 300 pixels inserted at the upper right of all posts, for example. As mentioned in Chapter 5, building your digital library is more important than ever, and blogging is one of the reasons why. You can also do a quick Google Image or Flickr Creative Commons search if you have nothing in-house to use. If you are featuring a video in the body of your blog post, most often you don't need an additional image in the upper right. That said, if readers have to scroll down more than one screen to see the video, then you should add an image to the top of the post as well.

11. If Your Blog Is Not Hosted inside Your Website, Purchase a Blog URL

It's a best practice to embed your blog within your website (such as one.org/blog), but many nonprofits won't have the capacity or tech know-how required to do that. That's OK. The ROI from blogging is still exceptionally high, even if your blog is not hosted inside your website. However, if it is not, the nonprofit should buy an additional URL to better promote its blog. For example, Nonprofit Tech 2.0 (nonprofitorgs.wordpress.com) has an alternative URL of nonprofit orgsblog.org for consistency in branding and promotion of the "nonprofitorgs" username. URLs usually cost less than $10 a year, and having them automatically forward to your blog is free. Some nonprofits even use a blog as their primary website, such as First Friday Art Walk in Springfield, Missouri. Its URL (ffaw.org) automatically forwards to a WordPress.com blog, and it has no additional website. For some small nonprofits on a tiny budget, that's a smart choice.

FIVE MUST-HAVE CHARACTERISTICS OF A NONPROFIT BLOGGER

A good nonprofit blogger doesn't need to be a professional writer or have years of experience writing for the Web, but he should enjoy writing, have a working knowledge of proper grammar, and invest time in improving his blogging skills and finding his blogger voice. Ideally, your nonprofit's primary blogger also serves as your social media manager for consistency in voice and cross-promoting content. However, nonprofits often have multiple bloggers to help share the responsibility and add variety to their blog content. Most blogging platforms allow for multiple authors, each with her own unique avatar and identity. That said, your nonprofit's primary blogger must have the following characteristics.

1. Be Confident

A blogger needs to be comfortable expressing her opinions online. Even if the opinion is not controversial, leadership and a solid sense of self are required for blogging. Some people just do not have the personality necessary to be public and open to criticism.

2. Be Disciplined

A blogger must have the discipline necessary to control the impulse to argue fervently with those who disagree with him. If a contrary comment is posted on your blog, let it sit for 24 hours and see whether your readers challenge the commenter. A good blogger has to develop a thick skin and can't take every contrary comment personally. That's easier said than done, but the last thing you want is your blogger flaming and indulging in arguments on your blog. Remember, it's best to delete and block disrespectful and blatantly rude people in social media, but you must allow civil debate and free speech. After 24 hours, if necessary, respond to the comment courteously with an intelligent rebuttal and leave it at that. Don't let the rare contrarian overtake you or your blog.

3. Be Organized

Blogging requires strong organizational skills. You often have to schedule interviews and blog assignments weeks in advance. You should be in the habit of regularly drafting ideas for future blog posts. To make sure that there is never a lull in publishing content, you always need to be thinking ahead. Also, managing digital photos and video content for blog posts requires organizational skills, as does distributing blog content to various social networking and mobile communities. A person who is easily overwhelmed by details will struggle with blogging.

4. Have SEO Knowledge

Every blog post is an opportunity to increase your nonprofit's SEO. A good blogger will know what keywords and phrases to use, be able to monitor search results, and have a basic understanding of SEO. Sadly, lack of SEO knowledge is common in the nonprofit blogging community.

5. Enjoy Social Media

Blogging is social media. Responding to comments graciously and with patience is required from a nonprofit blogger. She must also have the skills and passion necessary to seed her blog content throughout social networking communities.

ELEVEN BLOG CONTENT IDEAS FOR NONPROFITS

Thanks to the Social Web, there is no shortage of possible topics for your nonprofit to blog about. From 10-paragraph editorials to 2-paragraph commentaries on breaking news, when you use the ideas given here, you should have no problem publishing the required minimum of one blog post per week (less than that and your blog starts to look abandoned). Still, understand that the more good, high-quality content your nonprofit blog publishes, the higher your ROI. That said, mix it up! Post a wide variety of blog content, and have some fun with it. Finally, remember that blog posts make great content for e-newsletters. Definitely integrate your blog posts with your e-newsletter.

1. Share and Comment on Breaking News

One of the more effective ways to generate buzz for and traffic to your blog is to tap into the breaking news cycle. If a news story is breaking when you get to work in the morning, and it is related to your mission or your programs, write up a quick two-paragraph summary of or commentary about the breaking news story, add a link to the original source, and then distribute your blog post to your communities. People are much more responsive and likely to share your blog post if its subject matter is related to a breaking news story. Most nonprofits distribute the original source of the story to their communities (the *New York Times*, for example), but while that is generous, it does not help build the nonprofit's brand recognition, e-newsletter list, or social networking communities; rather, it builds those of the *New York Times*. That said, you should be careful not to become a breaking news spammer by overusing this strategy, but you will discover that some of your most trafficked blog posts will be related to breaking news.

2. Post Calls to Action

Often tied to breaking news stories or internal developments at your organization, a blog post calling for action is often well received. A call to action can be an urgent donation pitch, a request to sign an online petition, or a call for volunteers. It's amazing what your supporters will be willing and able to do for your nonprofit if you just ask.

3. Share Stories, Photos, and Videos from Events

You should be regularly photographing and recording videos at important events that your nonprofit hosts. A day or two after the event, write up a brief blog post summarizing the event, with a Flickr slideshow or YouTube video recapping the event. It's also good to feature quotes from supporters who attended the event. Quite often, a good slideshow or video will entice supporters to give priority to attending your next event.

4. Provide Organizational Updates

If your nonprofit is launching a new program or campaign, definitely write a blog post to share the news and summarize the new program or campaign's goals. Your supporters will probably help to share the news and provide valuable feedback. Organizational updates can also include announcements of conferences or fundraisers, staff changes, or any recent awards or accolades your nonprofit has received. It's also a good idea that every time you launch a new social media or mobile technology community or campaign, you write a brief blog post and list specific ways in which supporters can participate. If you start using QR codes, write a blog post explaining how you will use them. If you launch a new Foursquare campaign, write about that, too. Again, you'll be surprised by what your supporters will do to help your nonprofit online if you just keep them informed.

5. Share Stories from the Field

For nonprofits that have staff members or volunteers in the field, definitely encourage them to send in reports with photos for blog posts. A first-person voice is best. Nonprofits that work in international development, disaster relief, or wildlife conservation often do this sort of storytelling in print materials and website articles, but it also works extremely well as blog content. Another idea is to have staff members send in reports from important conferences, meetings, or protests.

6. Interview Experts

A 10-question blog interview with an expert in an area related to your nonprofit's mission and programs can be interesting to your supporters. Interview a professor, government official, or esteemed professional, such as a scientist, social worker, activist, or artist. Be sure to insert and bold the questions in the blog post, keep answers limited to two or three paragraphs, and always include the expert's photo. The easiest way to conduct these interviews is through e-mail or over the phone, but for the enterprising blogger with a penchant for journalism, in-person interviews provide the opportunity to get action photos and video interviews.

7. Allow Guest Bloggers to Post Commentary and Share Their Expertise

Additionally, you can ask experts to write guest blog posts. Some will be too busy to take the time to write, but others will happily embrace the opportunity. Your role is to give them a word limit, a general topic, and a deadline, and to solicit photos. Since there's always the possibility that a guest blogger will be a poor writer or controversial in his subject matter or tone, it's best to ask experts who are already closely connected to your nonprofit.

8. Share Resources and Useful Tips

Blog posts that share resources and useful tips are some of the most popular on the Social Web. For example, if you are a health nonprofit, write a post about foods that help lower blood pressure, or provide tips on how to exercise at home. If you are an environmental nonprofit, write about ways in which supporters can green their homes or garden without pesticides. If you are a nonprofit that works with low-income communities, write blog posts that share recipes for low-cost meals and energy-saving tips. Newspapers and magazines publish these sorts of articles regularly because they generate buzz. There's no reason why nonprofits can't capture some of that buzz, too.

9. Solicit Feedback and Direction from Supporters

When you are considering launching a new campaign or starting a new online community, go to the blogosphere for advice. Just be prepared to listen to people's feedback! Let's say you are considering investing in a text-to-give campaign, and you are about ready to sign the contract. Before you do, write a blog post asking your readers if they have any interest in donating to your nonprofit via text, and why or why not? They will surely let you know, either through an onslaught of feedback or through a defining, all-telling silence. It cannot be stressed enough that your supporters are eager to be engaged and useful, but you need to open your nonprofit to their feedback and direction. It's also worth pointing out that if you can get your supporters engaged in a new program or campaign during the idea stage, they are very likely to assist throughout the launch and implementation stages as well.

10. Write Numbered Lists

Numbered lists are the most retweeted, liked, and shared blog posts on the Social Web today. Seriously! Some of the most successful blogs on the Web today regularly publish blog posts with numbered lists, and once you start, you will quickly notice that these posts are becoming your most trafficked blog posts. Some examples for nonprofits are "10 Ways You Can Help Fight Poverty," "Four Reasons Why the Green Economy Is America's Future Economy," "10 Tips to Help You Quit Smoking," and "Eight Benefits of Volunteering." Your nonprofit should set a goal of publishing a minimum of four lists per year, and it's worth noting that these lists make great content for e-newsletters as well.

11. Highlight Special Donors, Fundraisers, and Volunteers

Blogs are a great platform for highlighting donors, fundraisers, volunteers, and other supporters through "of the month" posts. These posts help your nonprofit show appreciation to your most valuable supporters and create an incentive for other supporters to do and give more. Though most of them won't come right out and say it, many people appreciate public recognition for their contribution. It makes them feel special and important. These posts can also be very effective in e-newsletters. Keep them brief, include a quote or two from the person being highlighted, and definitely add his picture.

WHAT ABOUT CATEGORIES AND TAGS?

Many nonprofit blogs use categories and tags to organize blog posts into lists or clouds for easy navigation and browsing of archived blog posts. These are confusing to a lot of bloggers, but the easiest way to think of them is that categories are file folders with general topics (like Environment) and tags are the contents of those folders (Habitat Loss, Global Warming, Pollution). Each blog post should be added to a primary category (for navigation) and then tagged (for easy browsing) by issue or subject. A blog post will probably have many tags but just one category.

It's best if you map out your categories and tags when you first launch your blog and then use them consistently in each blog post you publish. If your nonprofit is late to categories and tags, you should go back and categorize and tag your most trafficked posts, then use them for every post in the future. However, if you want to keep it simple, choose one over the other (categories over tags) and just leave it at that.

FINAL WORDS:
BLOGS ARE GOING MOBILE

By 2015, your supporters will probably be reading your blog posts on mobile devices more often than on desktop computers. In fact, blog platforms and blog content are increasingly becoming the foundation of a rapidly evolving Mobile Web. Even if the idea of mobile communications and fundraising feels overwhelming and distant, take solace in knowing that launching a blog for your nonprofit today is also a crucial first step in launching a successful mobile communications and fundraising strategy tomorrow. If your nonprofit wants to tap into the power of early adoption and be a leader in mobile technology, then now is the time to launch or relaunch your blog.

Nonprofit Examples of Excellence

- *A Nun's Life* blog: anunslife.org/blog

- *Charity: water* blog: charitywater.org/blog

- Global Exchange blogs: globalexchange.org/blogs

- LIVESTRONG blog: livestrongblog.org

- Oxfam International blogs: blogs.oxfam.org

Google This!

- ❏ Nonprofitorgsblog.org

- ❏ Blogpulse.com

- ❏ Wikipedia meta tags

- ❏ Top 10 reviews blogging services

- ❏ Wordpress for nonprofits: the complete guide

- ❏ Premiumwp.com

- ❏ Dosomething.org

WEB 3.0
THE MOBILE WEB

SOCIAL MEDIA AND THE MOBILE WEB

Don't expect a long URL on an outdoor ad to attract many visitors, no matter how passionate or creative your ad is. People simply behave differently on mobile devices than they do on their home computers. If you want them to take action, give them something they can realistically do on their mobiles in a short amount of time—check in on a location-based app, scan a QR code, text-to-give—otherwise, your outdoor ad will just be another pretty picture.

—Ray Wan, manager of marketing and design, Earthjustice

WEB 3.0 IS THE BRAVE NEW FRONTIER IN COMMUNICATIONS AND FUNDRAISING

Just as social media has transformed nonprofit communications and fundraising, so will the Mobile Web. If you thought Web 2.0 was overwhelming, then get ready to be absolutely deluged with a wave of new mobile tools over the next few years. The Web is moving faster than ever and shows absolutely no sign of slowing down. In fact, a report released in 2010 by Morgan Stanley predicts that based on the current rate of adoption, the Mobile Web is likely to be bigger than desktop Internet use by 2015. Nonprofits have a very important role to serve as mobile technology evolves, and some of the early adopters in the nonprofit sector have already begun to lead the way.

The Mobile Web is full of promise and potential for social good. It will connect communities worldwide in ways that the nonprofit sector has never experienced or even imagined. In the past, nonprofits in developing nations and the communities they serve have been hindered by the cost of desktop computers and Internet access; they often have not had the infrastructure in place or the financial capacity to utilize the Internet on a regular basis. The revolution in mobile technology in the developing world is changing that forever. Mobile phones are enabling many nonprofits and communities throughout the world to access the Internet regularly for the first time. There is still a long way to go, but tremendous progress has been made in recent years.

Ironically, the adoption of mobile technology by nonprofits in developed nations has taken longer, probably because it's more of a luxury than a necessity. BlackBerry and Palm pioneered the Mobile Web in the United States, but it wasn't until the release of the first iPhone in June 2007 (at a starting price of $499) that technophiles and Apple lovers caught smartphone fever en masse and helped usher in a new era of communications in the United States that has since spread worldwide. Since then, a mobile operating system known as Android (owned by Google) has come to market and is installed on smartphones with more affordable price points, and thus it has now surpassed the iPhone operating system as the number one smartphone operating system worldwide. While it's beneficial to know the history of smartphone technology, it's not crucial to your nonprofit's success with mobile communications. What matters most is that you have a smartphone, any smartphone, because without one, your nonprofit is missing out on an incredible opportunity to trailblaze the Mobile Web for social good.

THE BIG PICTURE: MOBILE SOCIAL NETWORKING AND LOCATION-BASED COMMUNITIES

Naturally, the proliferation of smartphones has resulted in an explosion of mobile social networking tools and location-based communities. From mobile photo-sharing services to live-streaming apps, what nonprofits can do with a smartphone and a little creativity is nothing less than phenomenal. Yet most nonprofits haven't even pondered the coming shift from desktop to mobile and how it will affect nonprofit communications and fundraising, especially if their staff members do not regularly use a smartphone in their personal lives.

Just as young people led the way with social media in 2005 and 2006, they are doing the same thing today with mobile technology. Teens and Millennials live and breathe mobile communications. It's hard for them to fathom not having a smartphone. That said, older adults are adopting this technology quickly, and as a result, the transition to the Mobile Web is occurring much more smoothly than the transition from the Static Web to the Social Web. It's also worth noting that in the United States, minorities are very active on the Mobile Web. Race and class raised their ugly heads in the Myspace vs. Facebook debate, and nonprofits should make a concerted effort to consider how race and class play a role on the Mobile Web in the coming years and shape their communications and development strategies accordingly.

Nonprofits have now been using social media long enough to have achieved a baseline of knowledge about what tools and best practices are most beneficial. That's not the case with mobile social networking tools and location-based communities. Now is the time for early adoption and experimentation. So, if your nonprofit is fortunate enough to have a social media manager who is excited by the prospect of the Mobile Web, then by all means necessary empower her to pioneer mobile technology on your nonprofit's behalf.

ELEVEN ESSENTIAL TOOLS FOR THE MOBILE SOCIAL MEDIA MANAGER

The best social media managers will embrace mobile technology and commit to being connected and communicating with their communities from anywhere at any time when the need arises. Whether we like it or not, in the future, the working schedule of nonprofit communicators will no longer be limited to Monday through Friday, 9 to 5. The emerging leaders of the nonprofit sector will function much like reporters on call. They will tweet from location, break news on Facebook, send out group text calls to action, document with real-time photos and videos, and even broadcast live from events as they unfold. Some nonprofits have begun to lay a foundation for their mobile social networking and location-based strategies. Most haven't even considered mobile communications. The tools listed here will help you get started.

1. A Smartphone!

Whether everyone in the communications and development office or just the social media manager has a smartphone, it is now a necessary piece of hardware for nonprofits. Staff members should not be required to use their personal smartphones and data plans for work reasons—unless they want to. A smartphone is necessary if the social media manager is to be able to experiment with mobile social networking tools, location-based services, mobile websites, and group text messaging. You'll need hands-on experience on a regular basis. If a smartphone is not already in your nonprofit's budget, write it in for next year. You'll want to allocate at least $100 a month for a smartphone, or reimburse your social media manager a percentage of her mobile and data plan if she is willing to use hers. However, in the long run, it is better to have a smartphone with only your nonprofit's mobile history and activity on it, rather than one on which your activity is mixed with your social media manager's personal life.

CNET.com and TopTenREVIEWS.com offer annual reviews of the best smartphones on the market. You should make it a priority to get a smartphone that has a good still-shot camera, a video camera, and high speed. Backing up your smartphone contacts, messages, images, and videos also needs to become a part of your regular routine. Most smartphones will cost $100 to $200 when you sign a contract with a carrier. If you don't want to sign a contract, you can purchase a smartphone for full price ($200 to $600) and go to a local discount wireless provider.

Some mobile social media managers will need more than a smartphone can offer. Typing on a smartphone can be difficult. If you plan on blogging or writing any content longer than a sentence or two, then you'll probably want to invest in a tablet as well. It's entirely possible that you'll soon be able to make phone calls and text from tablets, so a tablet may be something to add to your budget. The use of tablets, especially the iPad, is exploding, and there is likely to be a great deal of innovation in tablets in coming years.

2. A Facebook App

The number of people that use Facebook on a mobile device is now growing faster than the number using it on a desktop. Odds are that a good percentage of your nonprofit's Facebook status updates are being read on smartphones and tablets at all different times of the day from many locations. Knowing that, a good social media manager is always alert and thinking about his mission and his communities, and important news or inspiration quite often does not come during normal working office hours. For the social media manager on the go, that means that he'll need an easy way to update your communities— for example, while on the bus on the way home from work, on his lunch break, at the airport, from a conference, or even in the evening while watching TV. He'll have balance, but he'll also understand that this is part of his job description now.

Facebook has a suite of tools that enables you to access your nonprofit's Facebook Page easily from anywhere at any time. Go to facebook.com/mobile, where you can either download Facebook's smartphone app(s) or find out more information about its mobile site at m.facebook.com.

3. A Twitter App

Twitter is a much faster community than Facebook, and because of that, it's likely that you'll be tweeting on your smartphone more often than you'll be posting status updates on your Facebook Page. There are hundreds of mobile apps specialized for Twitter. To make it easy, start by using Twitter's official app, found by going to its mobile website at m.twitter.com. The site will detect your smartphone automatically and provide a link to download the appropriate Twitter app.

From there, you can experiment with third-party Twitter apps like HootSuite or TweetDeck, which also allow you to update your Facebook Page, Twitter Profile, and Foursquare account. However, downloading the official apps from each social network and using them individually has its advantages. They are always the most current and extremely well built, and apps like HootSuite and TweetDeck, while incredibly enticing in theory, do run the risk of giving your friends, followers, and fans the impression that you are an automated marketing robot living in a HootSuite or TweetDeck bubble. Only the best social media managers and community builders can use tools like HootSuite and TweetDeck and resist the temptation to automate content.

4. A Foursquare (or Gowalla, Yelp, or Google Places) App

An increasing number of social media managers will be checking in on location-based communities like Foursquare and Gowalla to promote their nonprofit. All these communities have a suite of smartphone apps that are compatible with numerous smartphones and mobile websites. Nowhere is the line between the personal and the professional in technology more blurred than when participating in location-based communities, so even though early adoption of such services is smart, checking in is not for everyone. For those who are comfortable participating in location-based communities, downloading and using the official apps is a must because the tool sets offered by these sites are constantly being upgraded.

5. A Mobile Photo-Sharing App

The number of mobile photo-sharing apps is exploding, and nonprofits are increasingly embracing the trend. Telling your nonprofit's story through digital photography while the story is still unfolding is proving to be a very effective means of inspiring and engaging your communities on social networking sites. In addition to Twitter Photos, TwitPic, and yfrog, there are also DailyBooth, Hipstamatic, and Instagram, which allow instantaneous editing, text overlay, and special effects using color and borders. A social media manager with an enthusiasm for digital photography and a creative eye can have a lot of fun with mobile photo-sharing.

6. A Mobile Video-Sharing App

Similarly, if you have a smartphone with a video recorder, your nonprofit can easily record and share videos with your social networking communities from anywhere at any time using Twitter Videos, TwitVid, or yfrog. As more mobile devices come to have video recorders installed, this trend will evolve quickly, and the number of services and tool sets available will expand quickly. Vimeo, Viddy,

Thwapr, and Qik are video hosting and mobile sharing tools that are worth exploring and experimenting with as well.

7. USTREAM (or Livestream)

Broadcasting live from a conference, a protest, or even Capitol Hill is one of the most cutting-edge areas in nonprofit communications today. The first step is to create a channel on a site like USTREAM or Livestream. The channel can be customized to match the branding of your nonprofit and can be configured to enable live tweets and Facebook status updates while you broadcast. Next, download the channel's smartphone app, which transforms the video recorder on your smartphone into a live video and audio broadcasting camera. Finally, start experimenting with and planning broadcast programs. You can launch weekly "TV" programs and/or report "Live!" from events. As wireless speeds continue to grow faster and Internet TV spreads to living rooms and thatched-roof dwellings worldwide, this is a trend that has huge potential and broad implications for nonprofit communications and fundraising.

8. A Mobile Browser

Mobile browsing (and thus mobile websites) is increasing rapidly in popularity. Smartphones come installed with a default browser, but you should also download and experiment with Opera Mini or Skyfire. They allow you to create a dashboard of favorite sites bookmarked for easy reference and enable easy content sharing on social networking sites. Also, if your nonprofit is creating a mobile website, you should test it on multiple mobile browsers.

9. A Mobile Payment App

The ability to accept credit card donations directly on your smartphone at fundraisers will fuel unprecedented amounts of donations being made at silent auctions, galas, protests, and marathons. Most people just don't carry cash and checkbooks anymore, and because of that, in-person fundraising campaigns have suffered, but thanks to recent innovations in mobile payment technology, your nonprofit can now easily accept donations anywhere at any time at a minimal cost directly through your smartphone.

Services like Square (squareup.com) and Intuit GoPayment (gopayment.com) allow you to install credit card payment readers directly on your smartphone, enabling simple swipe technology for payment processing. PayPal Mobile (paypal.com/mobile) is pioneering mobile payment technology with its smartphone apps and bump technology, which allows two iPhones to simply "bump" one another to carry out a payment transaction. Also, if your nonprofit has a mobile website with a "Donate Now" page that is optimized for mobile browsers, that could work just as well for processing donations while on the go.

10. A Group Texting App

Staff members and volunteers should consider staying in touch via group texting, especially during special events and campaigns. TextPlus is an app that is compatible with all smartphones and that allows you to text small groups of individuals for free. Members can text one another via "Reply All" or inside text "Communities." They can even share photos. Other similar services that also offer Web-based group management are Brightkite, Fast Society, and GroupMe. Groups are usually limited to 25 members or less, but in time these services may also begin to offer the ability to group text message large numbers of people at a low cost, or even free. Group texting services are still in their infancy and are definitely worth keeping an eye on over the next few years. In time, they could offer a wide range of mobile tools and functionality.

11. A QR Code Reader App

To experience how nonprofits are using quick response (QR) codes for awareness and fundraising campaigns, you are of course going to need a QR code reader app. Simply go to your app store/gallery and search for "qr code reader." Any free QR code reader will do.

INTRODUCTION TO LOCATION-BASED COMMUNITIES

In recent years, a wave of location-based communities, such as Facebook Places, Foursquare, and Gowalla, has hit the Internet and garnered a great deal of buzz in the blogosphere. Essentially, these communities are mobile social networks that are location-based and used primarily on smartphones. Empowered by geolocation technology, they can determine a user's physical location, thus enabling her to "check in" to a location while she is physically at that location. Location-based communities are popular mostly with users aged 18 to 29; the vast majority of Internet users have been slow to adopt them. Many individuals are uncomfortable with broadcasting their location to friends. That's a reasonable concern. Location-based communities are not for everyone.

However, with the integration of Facebook Places into the Facebook community and the rise of real-time content sharing, the idea of location-based social networking and "checking in" for social good is gaining momentum. If your nonprofit is location-based, you can opt not to use the services personally, but you can't ignore the "Places," "Venue," or "Spot" pages created by the users of location-based communities. Odds are that if your nonprofit is of one of the types listed here, then you probably already have places, venue, and spot pages on Facebook Places, Foursquare, and Gowalla:

- Museums and art galleries

- Libraries

- Performing arts venues and theaters

- Animal shelters, zoos, and aquariums

- Food banks and homeless shelters

- Health clinics, hospitals, and gyms

- Outdoor recreation venues

- Thrift stores and nonprofit retailers

- Schools and universities

- Churches and religious institutions

The fastest way to discover whether your nonprofit already has a presence on these sites is to do a Google search with the name of your nonprofit and the service—for example, search "museum of modern art foursquare." If you find that your nonprofit does indeed have places, venue, or spot page(s) and they are unclaimed, then you can sign up to claim them, which enables you to add content and special promotions to the pages. If you do not, then it's wise for you to join the sites and create places, venue, and spot pages for your nonprofit before someone else does it for you. There's a right way to do it and a wrong way to do it, and the general public, although well-intentioned, often sets up places, venue, and spot page(s) for nonprofits incorrectly.

FACEBOOK PLACES

Facebook Places is a location-based service that is integrated into the Facebook community. Using this service, which was launched in August 2010, Facebook users can check in on their smartphones to share with their Facebook friends where they are and to see if any of their friends are nearby. It's also touted as a tool that helps users "discover new places and things to do." When a Facebook user opens Facebook Places on his smartphone, he will see a list of places nearby and can then browse for the location where he wants to check in from. If it is not listed, then he can easily "Add a Place," which then creates a places page for that place. Facebook Places is a location-based community that grows organically as users add new places, check in, and upload photos to places pages. Your nonprofit can have an active presence on Facebook Places completely without your knowledge.

How to Claim Your Facebook Places Page

The first step is to discover whether or not your nonprofit has a places page. Unlike with Foursquare and Gowalla, where Google is the easiest way to find your page, for Facebook Places you need to attempt to check in, either on your Facebook smartphone app or on m.facebook.com, while you are physically present at your nonprofit. If you find the page, check in. It will then be posted to your personal profile on Facebook for later reference. If you do not find a page for your nonprofit, then "Add" your nonprofit to create a page and then check in.

Next, go to your Facebook Places Page at Facebook.com (not the mobile website or from your smartphone) and click "Is this your business?" You will then be prompted to claim your business. You must go through a process of verifying that you are an official representative of the place. Once you have been verified and approved, you can upload your nonprofit's avatar and add contact information. You are also given the option to explore purchasing advertising and participating in "Charity Deals" on the Facebook Places platform. Please see the Facebook Help Center for detailed information about Facebook Deals.

Finally, you are also provided the option of merging your Facebook Places Page with your official Facebook Page. That's extremely beneficial to nonprofits that are location-based, such as museums, libraries, and zoos, because people who have liked your places page are combined with those who have liked your official Facebook Page, instantaneously growing your fan base. Merging also adds a map (if you choose) of your location to your merged page, displays check-ins and likes, and is housed under the username you originally set for your official Facebook Page. However, the merging functionality was temporarily disabled at the time that this book went to print to remedy technical problems that arose for some during the merging process. Please research the subject of merging your places page with your official Facebook Page thoroughly before doing so, provided that Facebook reenables the merging option.

To Check In to Facebook Places or Not?

If you use your personal Facebook profile for work or for building your personal brand (that is, if you accept most friend requests that you receive), then checking in to your nonprofit's location regularly with status updates could be beneficial in the sense that you are promoting your nonprofit to your friends on Facebook. However, if you use your personal Facebook profile mostly to stay in touch with real friends and family members, then go easy on the check-ins. Most likely your friends are not that interested in seeing that you have shown up at work every day. For most nonprofits, the power of Facebook Places is in the Facebook Places Page itself. It's best to monitor and utilize upgrades in the Facebook Places tool set as they unfold and encourage your supporters to check in, like, and add photos to your places page.

FOURSQUARE

Foursquare was launched in March 2009, and within months it had usurped the online buzz of its competitors and become an instant favorite of the blogosphere. Unlike Gowalla at the time, you could easily "Add Venues" for locations to Foursquare during check-ins or on its desktop site. This subtle difference in functionality compelled the early adopters to join Foursquare and go on a binge of adding venues that they could then check in to and hope that by doing so, they could elevate themselves to the rank of "Mayor." Fueled by very simple game dynamics, Foursquare users earn points and "Badges" for adding venues and "Tips," for checking in, and for becoming mayors. Although this may seem silly to newcomers, mayorships and badges are much coveted by the Foursquare community, especially if they are hard to earn. Being the mayor of a popular venue has its popularity perks, and badges are prominently displayed on Foursquare profiles in "Trophy

Cases." This unique tool set propelled Foursquare to hit one million users by its one-year anniversary, and by the middle of 2011, it had surpassed ten million users. In the world of Internet start-ups, that is considered a phenomenal growth rate.

Since then, Gowalla has made it possible to "Create Spots" while checking in on smartphones, which has made it more enticing. Facebook Places was launched with the ability to add places from day one. That said, in terms of users, it is going to be difficult for Foursquare (and Gowalla) to compete with Facebook Places simply because of the size of the Facebook community. However, as mentioned early in this book, it's wise to diversify your online presence across many platforms. Facebook Places may have more users, but that doesn't mean that Foursquare is not valuable to your nonprofit. The two are completely different communities, each with its own unique tool set and purposes. Comparing the two is like comparing apples to oranges, or Facebook to Twitter. They are just different.

How to Claim Your Foursquare Venue Page

If your nonprofit is location-based, then it's likely that you already have a venue page on Foursquare. To claim it, you must first create a personal profile at foursquare.com/signup. You can sign up using your personal Facebook account or your e-mail address. If you sign up using your e-mail address, then use your real first and last names and be sure to link your new Foursquare Profile with your nonprofit's Twitter account. If your nonprofit does not have a Twitter account, then create one, because your Twitter username then becomes your Foursquare URL (foursquare.com/nonprofitorgs). However, do not automate Foursquare check-ins to Twitter or Facebook. You don't want to clutter your personal Facebook account or your nonprofit's Twitter feed with robotic check-ins. That said, it's worth noting that you can change your Foursquare URL at a later date, which is likely if you decide to create a Foursquare business page. Finally, use a personal photo with your nonprofit's Twibbon (foursquare.com/nonprofitorgs) for your new Foursquare Profile. Using your nonprofit's avatar for a

Foursquare Profile crosses that thin line between authenticity and over-the-top marketing and can easily do more harm than good to your nonprofit's brand.

Next, conduct a Google search to locate your nonprofit's venue page (or use foursquare.com/search). Once you have located it, select "Do you manage this venue? Claim here" and follow the instructions for claiming your venue page. Once you have claimed it, you can then update contact information, create "Specials," and view statistical information about your venue page and its visitors. If you can't find a venue page for your nonprofit, you can easily create one (foursquare.com/add_venue) and then claim it. If you are a location-based nonprofit, consider offering a special. For example, the Atlanta History Center offers $2 off an admission ticket when Foursquare users check in for the first time, and the Phoenix Zoo offers $1 off admission for every canned food item brought in, which is then donated to St. Mary's Food Bank. Foursquare specials pop up on smartphones when users check in to venues in the vicinity of your location, helping your nonprofit get greater exposure on Foursquare and tangible results.

Finally, download the Foursquare app to your smartphone or use its mobile website (m.foursquare.com) to check in. Do so while you are physically at your nonprofit's location, and then do it again the next day to become the mayor of your venue page so that your page is not mayorless. After that, let the mayor wars begin.

How to Create a Foursquare Business Page for Your Nonprofit

For nonprofits that are not primarily location-based, Foursquare launched the ability to create "Business Pages" for brands. Rather than people friending your business page, they "Follow" your page in order to see tips (which pop up after check-ins on smartphones) that you have posted in your city, your country, or even around the world. Business pages can be branded to match your nonprofit's website and can also include links to your website, blog, Facebook Page, and/or Twitter Profile. Business pages also include the ability to check in to venue pages and post photos to venues as your nonprofit. For those who do not want to check in personally on Foursquare, business pages are a great alternative. For example, People for the Ethical Treatment of Animals (PETA) has a Foursquare Business Page (foursquare.com/peta) where it offers tips on animal welfare, check-ins to restaurants, and photos of vegetarian and vegan food. Brands that have business pages also have the capability to create badges, but only a limited few are selected. You can learn more and sign up to create a business page at foursquare.com/business/brands.

Although this may be a bit confusing, many nonprofits have both a venue page and a business page. Venue pages are central hubs where Foursquare users check in and leave their own tips, and business pages are meant to enable brands to check in and post their own tips as well. Having both types of pages does not negatively affect your brand inside the Foursquare community; it does, however, confuse nonprofits concerning which page they should promote. Since your venue page automatically pops up during check-ins, it is best to promote your business page on your website, blog, e-newsletter, and other such places. It's also a good idea to link to your venue page on your business page.

To Check In to Foursquare or Not?

If you weren't confused already, there's a third option for using Foursquare to promote your nonprofit, and that's checking in using your personal profile on Foursquare as long as you have not converted it into a profile for your nonprofit. Foursquare launched business pages in response to the fact that tens of thousands of brands, of their own free will, started converting personal profiles into profiles for brands and then started sending friend requests en masse to Foursquare users. Although Foursquare enabled mass friending for almost two years to get the early adopters engaged and active, in January 2011, it started limiting the number of friend requests that personal profiles can send on any given day. It had to. Friend requests from brands (such as, "Jean Company, Inc., wants to be your friend") feel spammish, and as Myspace taught us, nothing kills a social network faster than spam.

Whether you want to check in, leave tips, and post "Shouts" with the personal profile you created to claim your Venue Page is your choice. If there is a personality at your nonprofit that is well known, public, and willing to use her real name, she would be ideal for a personal profile on Foursquare. However you decide to use Foursquare (or not), at the very least you must claim your venue page. That's easy. From there, the best way to grasp Foursquare's extensive tool set is to just start checking in. It will become clear sooner rather than later whether you personally feel comfortable using Foursquare and whether you think it's beneficial for your nonprofit for you to invest your time and resources beyond claiming your venue page.

GOWALLA

Like Foursquare, Gowalla was launched in March 2009. Since then, there's been much Gowalla vs. Foursquare debate and comparisons, but although both are location-based communities, they are quite different and distinct from each other in terms of their design and their tool set. That said, Gowalla is in third place in terms of users, behind Facebook Places and Foursquare. The subtle difference that initially Gowalla users could not create spots on Gowalla's desktop website or through Gowalla's mobile website, but only from an iPhone app, made it less interesting and accessible to many early adopters. Simply checking in and earning "Stamps" and "Pins" wasn't enough to keep them engaged, and even though Gowalla pioneered the ability to add photos to spots and to comment on check-ins, that wasn't enough either. People want to help build the community too by creating and editing spot pages. Gowalla's initial decision to significantly limit users' ability to create spots cost it in terms of users and crippled its momentum in comparison to Foursquare.

Since then, Gowalla has made strides to compete. In reality, the site has much more to offer in terms of tools and functionality than its competitors. The ability to create "Trips" and "Events" was also pioneered by Gowalla, and although they are a bit more confusing, its stamp and pin game dynamics are multilayered and more generous. Gowalla also offers the ability to leave "Notes" and bookmark spots. Gowalla is distinctly different from Facebook Places and Foursquare, and it is too early to say with absolute certainty which site is the best investment of your nonprofit's time and resources. In fact, because of the volatile nature of start-ups, it's wise to diversify your brand and dabble with all three, especially if your nonprofit is location-based.

How to Claim Your Gowalla Spot Page

After you have located your nonprofit's spot page or created one, click "Claim It Now" on the desktop version of your spot page and simply follow the instructions. After your claim is approved, you can then edit your contact information and add a check-in message that pops up to your supporters when they check in to your spot on their smartphones. The message could be a call to action, a text-to-donate now pitch, or powerful stats related to your nonprofit's mission and programs. Additionally, your nonprofit can buy a custom "Passport Stamp" that users earn when they check in to your spot page. Gowalla has a team of skilled designers available that will design a stamp for your nonprofit or for an event. There is a waiting list, so you can learn more and sign up to be alerted when new stamps are available at gowalla.com/stamps.

To Check In to Gowalla or Not?

If your nonprofit has a spot page, then at the very least you should check in to add photos to your spot page. From there, you can also create trips that function like tours (ideal for art walks, historical societies, institutions of higher education, and similar organizations) and leave "Highlights." Gowalla also allows you to custom-design the background for your personal profile. As mentioned before, in terms of functionality and the depth of its tool set, it is way ahead of Facebook Places and Foursquare. It's a lot more colorful, and with each new tool launched, it's getting more interesting. If you are uncomfortable checking in using your real name on Gowalla, then use only your first name and your Twitter username as your last name, such as gowalla.com/nonprofitorgs (also possible on Foursquare). You can also request that Gowalla convert your personal profile into a business profile with "Follow" and passport functionality by emailing their business development department at business@gowalla.com. That said, there's a lot going on inside the Gowalla community, and once you start experimenting, you might discover that you enjoy checking in and dropping "Items." As most early adopters will tell you, pioneering new tools has its risks in terms of time spent and possibly lost, but it also has its payoffs.

GOOGLE PLACES, YELP, AND LOOPT?

Yes, yes, and yes—especially if your nonprofit is location-based. Google Places and Yelp were initially launched as ways to find out more information about a nonprofit or business through user-generated reviews and ratings, but in 2010, both added the ability to check in. Be sure to create a Google Places account (places.google.com/business) to access, edit, and utilize your Google Places page, and then download the Google Latitude app to check in. For Yelp, you need to "Unlock" your business page (yelp.com/business) to access its tool set. Loopt is another location-based community where users can create Loopt Places for a nonprofit. There's no mobile website version (yet) for check-ins, but you should download its app and check in to your places page to monitor your "Qs" (short for questions), photos, and total check-ins.

Now, while all these new location-based communities may seem overwhelming, the truth is that this is just the beginning. These communities will probably become integrated into social networking sites, mobile games (like SCVNGR and MyTown), and perhaps even group texting tools. It's hard to imagine how all this will evolve and function in five years, but the time to get invested is now. If your nonprofit is location-based, then you absolutely must get into the habit of regularly claiming and monitoring your places, venues, and spots on location-based communities and apps. You don't have a choice. The truth is that your nonprofit has or will have a presence on these sites, whether you want it to or not, and all signs point to further proliferation of location-based communities and services unique to the Mobile Web.

FIVE WAYS TO CHECK IN FOR GOOD

Now that you have claimed and accessed your nonprofit's pages on Facebook Places, Foursquare, Gowalla, Google Places, Yelp, and Loopt, it is time to start checking in for good and creating check-in campaigns that benefit your nonprofit. Let the creativity flow, and have some fun with it! There are no proven best practices, and the time is ripe for early adoption. Like the early adopters of Myspace, Facebook, and Twitter, there are nonprofits whose brand recognition will soar to new levels from being the first to cleverly and uniquely utilize location-based communities. Here are some ideas to get your nonprofit started.

1. Ask Your Supporters to Dedicate Their Check-Ins

When users check in on location-based communities, they can post status updates with their check-ins. Create a page on your website or blog asking your supporters to dedicate their check-ins to your non-profit by providing them examples of three or five short messages that they can post during check-ins. For example, "Earthjustice: Because the earth needs a good lawyer: m.twitter.com/earthjustice." Or, "Help Stop Cyberbullying! Visit m.cyberbullying.co.uk to learn more!" Or, "Support Our Troops! Like IAVA at m.facebook.com/iava.org."

2. Launch Check-In Campaigns for Events

There's an unlimited number of ways to use location-based communities for activism. People can check in en masse at the offices of politicians or at protests. Corporate accountability activists can check in and post tips and notes that educate consumers. You can also create incentives to check in at conference sessions and fundraisers like galas and marathons, and, of course, provide special discounts or rewards to check in to your nonprofit. The possibilities are vast, and the potential is as yet untapped.

3. Upload Photos with Your Nonprofit's Avatar to Places, Venues, and Spots in Your Area

This will seem a little strange to many nonprofit communicators, but you can create a 6- × 6-inch hard copy of your nonprofit's avatar with your mobile website URL printed on it and carry it with you. Then, when you check in around town, you can pull out the hard copy of your avatar and take and upload photos while on location to places, venues, or spots with your avatar featured in the photo. When people browse those locations on their smartphones, they will see the photos taken by your nonprofit with your avatar and mobile website URL. It doesn't get any more guerrilla marketing than that! The more photos of your avatar that you post, the more exposure your nonprofit gets.

4. Create a Check-In Speakers Tour

If your nonprofit has staff members who regularly give presentations or travel for work, have them check in, then promote their speaking tour check-ins using WeePlaces.com. Fun, and visually compelling!

5. Organize a Scavenger Hunt or Tour

Location-based communities make scavenger hunts and self-guided tours much easier to organize. They also provide a clever new fundraising option. Your supporters sign up by making a donation to participate and then create a scavenger hunt of check-ins or a city or art tour. This can be as simple as you'd like, or it can be a full-fledged campaign complete with traditional advertising, T-shirts, a tiered level of prizes, and sponsors for each check-in location.

FINAL WORDS:
PRIVACY IS NOT DEAD, JUST EVOLVING

As mobile social networking and location-based communities continue to proliferate, the privacy debate is going to become more heated and more complicated. Whatever your beliefs about privacy on the Internet or the lack thereof, the truth is that you must now be proactive if you are to protect your privacy online. It's not something that you can be passive about any longer. You have to monitor your privacy settings on social networking sites regularly, and when engaging in mobile social networking and utilizing location-based communities, some basic common sense will defuse most privacy concerns. That said, nonprofits are now in an unprecedented interdependent relationship with for-profit companies like Facebook, Twitter, Google, and Foursquare whose revenue models often depend on their getting access to your private information. You can't be too shocked when they sell your personal data to their customers, but you can actively take steps to prevent it provided you educate yourself on proper privacy settings and smart use of mobile technology. Nonprofits like the Electronic Frontier Foundation (eff.org) and the Electronic Privacy Information Center (epic.org) are there to help. Privacy is not dead as long as you are willing to take responsibility for it and take steps to protect it.

Nonprofit Examples of Excellence: Location-Based Communities

- Brooklyn Museum: facebook.com/brooklynmuseum

- Hopalong Animal Rescue: yelp.com/biz/hopalong-animal-rescue-oakland

- National Wildlife Federation: foursquare.com/nwf

- Springfield Regional Arts Council: gowalla.com/Springfield Arts

- UNICEF: twitpic.com/photos/unicef

Google This!

❏ Wikipedia mobile web

❏ Mobile technology for nonprofit organizations linkedin group

❏ Mobileactive.org

❏ Mobile web will dominate by 2015

❏ Youtube did you know 4.0

❏ Youtube the growth of mobile: stats and figures that will shock you

❏ Youtube the mobile world in figures

❏ Pewinternet.org

❏ Mobile web millennials

❏ Mobile web minorities

- ❏ Top 10 reviews smartphones
- ❏ Top 10 reviews tablets
- ❏ Mobile backup
- ❏ Freepress.net/freemyphone
- ❏ Wikipedia geolocation
- ❏ Facebook.com/places
- ❏ Merging facebook places
- ❏ Facebook.com/deals
- ❏ Foursquare.com/nonprofitorgs
- ❏ Aboutfoursquare.com
- ❏ Foursquare.com/business
- ❏ Foursquare app gallery
- ❏ Gowalla.com/nonprofitorgs
- ❏ Gowalla.com/business
- ❏ Places.google.com/business
- ❏ Google.com/latitude
- ❏ Yelp.com/business
- ❏ Dailyfeats.com

MOBILE WEBSITES

People increasingly expect to be able to access your nonprofit's information whenever and wherever on their mobile devices. When we first launched our mobile website in the fall of 2010, we learned quickly that our mobile site didn't have to be full-featured or expensive, but it did need to be useful. What we ended up with was Goodwill on the Go—a mobile-optimized site where people can find their local Goodwill, browse employment opportunities, or text-to-give directly from their mobile phone.

—*Adam Stiska, online media manager,*
Goodwill Industries International

THE BIG PICTURE: CREATING AND DISTRIBUTING CONTENT FOR THE MOBILE WEB

The rise of smartphones and tablets has dramatically transformed the way people consume and distribute content. You can now read news and blogs and do social networking from anywhere at any time. The problem is that much of that content is still formatted for desktop consumption, and reading it on mobile devices—especially on smartphones—is very challenging, if not impossible. Large media outlets and well-known blogs began to realize in 2009 that their Web content would have to be converted for easier consumption. The result was a rush of new smartphone apps, primarily for the iPhone. At the time, mobile websites were low on organizations' priority scale. The buzz was overwhelmingly about smartphone apps; tablets did not exist yet, and the number of people that were browsing mobile websites was small.

That began to change dramatically in 2010. Smartphone apps can be glitchy, and some frustrated users began to explore using mobile websites instead (m.nytimes.com, m.npr.org, and m.huffpost.com, for example). Also, as the smartphone market diversified, the growing need to launch numerous versions of a smartphone app (iPhone, BlackBerry, Android, and so on) sparked a new conversation about the value of mobile websites. Every smartphone and cell phone with a mobile browser can access a mobile website. It began to make more sense to invest time in designing and improving mobile websites than to invest it in launching and maintaining multiple versions of a smartphone app. Today, the number of users who access mobile websites on a daily basis continues to skyrocket, and as a result, mobile websites are increasingly becoming the foundation of successful Mobile Web campaigns.

FIVE REASONS WHY YOUR NONPROFIT NEEDS A MOBILE WEBSITE

For the most part, nonprofits have been slow to launch mobile websites. In 2009 and 2010, nonprofits were busy launching and improving their social media campaigns. The Mobile Web was on their to-do list, but it was relegated to 2011 and 2012. There were some early adopters, but for the most part nonprofits felt overwhelmed by the prospect of launching a mobile website. Thankfully, it's not that difficult or expensive, but first it's important to understand why your nonprofit needs a mobile website.

1. To Improve Your Group Text Messaging Campaigns

If your nonprofit is going to launch a group text messaging campaign, then you absolutely need a mobile website. Text messages are limited to 160 characters, and after a short while, text-only messages become boring to subscribers. You need to be able to send group text messages that link to Web pages where readers can "Learn More" or "Take Action," but it makes no sense to link to a Web page that was designed to be read on a 12- to 14-inch computer screen—that is, your desktop website. In group text messaging campaigns, you need to be able to link to mobile Web pages designed to be read quickly and efficiently on 3-inch or less smartphone screens.

2. To Make Your Smartphone Apps More Functional

In 2009 and 2010, many nonprofits rushed to launch smartphone apps. The impulse to be an early adopter is to be commended, but there was a huge disconnect in those years, as it makes little sense to link to a desktop website rather than a mobile website in a smartphone app. For a smartphone app to be fully functional, it needs to link to Web pages that were designed to be viewed through mobile browsers. There's little value in linking to your "Donate Now" desktop page through a smartphone app if a potential donor has to scroll right, left, up, and down and zoom in and zoom out just to fill out the required fields.

3. To Empower QR Code Campaigns

The increased use of QR codes in the nonprofit sector led to a lot of "Aha!" moments about the need for a mobile website. If nonprofits are going to ask supporters to use their smartphones to scan a QR code that links to a Web page, then of course the QR code needs to link to a mobile website.

4. To Improve Location-Based Community Campaigns

If your nonprofit is going to utilize location-based communities like Facebook Places, Foursquare, or Gowalla, then there will be times when you'll want a mobile website that you can mention and promote in check-ins and list on places, venue, or spot pages. The more these tools grow in popularity, the more obvious it will become that your nonprofit needs a mobile website.

5. To Optimize Mobile Search Engine Optimization

On the Mobile Web, it's 1999 all over again. Mobile browsers are hungry for new mobile content. It's a clean slate in terms of keyword and page title optimization. Get in now while the getting is still good!

LAUNCHING AND MAINTAINING A MOBILE WEBSITE

Compared to a desktop website, launching a mobile website is a breeze and much less expensive. With the tools that are available today, there is no reason to build or maintain a hard-coded mobile website. If you set it up correctly using your blog's RSS feed and a mobile content management system (CMS), a simple mobile website requires very little maintenance, is automatically optimized for mobile browsing and search, and costs as little as $100 a year. Although nonprofit vendors like Convio and Mobile Commons are ramping up their Mobile Web tool sets, for those nonprofits that can't afford them, there are some phenomenal, cost-effective alternatives.

- *MoFuse.* MoFuse.com is a mobile CMS. For as little as $8 a month, you can launch a simple mobile website with five customizable mobile Web pages ("About Us," "Take Action," "Subscribe," and so on). That price also includes mobilizing your blog content, meaning that MoFuse will automatically convert your blog posts into a format that is consistent with your mobile website design. You can also view stats, format colors and layout, and easily add images (such as a mobile website header and social networking icons). MoFuse even comes with a QR code manager that allows you to create and then track your QR code campaigns. To make the most of MoFuse, basic knowledge of HTML is required.

- *ur mobile.* Founded in 2009, urmobile.com is a mobile website vendor that solely serves the nonprofit sector. Using its do-it-yourself MobBuilder tool, you can quickly launch a well-designed website that can include RSS feeds, videos, slideshows, polls, and custom forms. Fees range from $60 to $270 monthly depending upon the size of your website, and for an additional $20 per month, you can create a mobile-optimized donation form. See m.komen.org for an example of a mobile website built using MobBuilder.

- *Mobify.* Mobify.me starts at more than $250 a month, and for most nonprofits that's not a necessary expense, but large international and national nonprofits that have more generous budgets should explore its tool set because Mobify is the top of the line in mobile CMS. That said, mobile CMS services are probably going to flood the market in the coming years, driving the price for such services way down. If in doubt, start small and inexpensive, just as long as you start!

Finally, when you are setting up your mobile website, it's best to opt for m.domainname.org over domainname.mobi, but depending upon what vendor you are using, that's not always possible. In that case, buy a ".mobi" URL from Register.com or Network Solutions and have it redirect to the default domain set up by your mobile CMS provider.

ELEVEN MOBILE WEBSITE DESIGN BEST PRACTICES FOR NONPROFITS

It's ironic how Web design has come full circle. In the 1990s, websites were utilitarian in appearance and structure. Slow dial-up Internet access required that websites be as simple as possible for faster loading. A basic banner at the top, nonimage links for navigation, and text pages with few photos were all that the Internet could handle. During the 2000s, with the rise of broadband, came an onslaught of highly designed websites with Flash and JavaScript, pop-down navigation, and pop-up windows for slideshows, videos, and calls to action. The evolution of Web design aesthetics over the last 10 to 15 years has been directly correlated with the increase in speed of Internet access. Today, for the exact same reason, we're starting from the beginning in mobile website design. Until we reach 5G or 6G speed, mobile websites will have to be very simple to avoid long, frustrating download times.

1. Keep Design and Navigation Simple

Navigation and secondary pages should be limited to five or fewer. Mobile users like things simple and can be overwhelmed by a multilayered mobile website. Be sure to feature a "Home" link prominently. Require only up and down scrolling, never left to right. The content background should be white with black text. You can add some color to your mobile website through navigation bars and images. It's also common to provide a link to your "Desktop" version in case the user has a tablet and wants to browse your "real" website. If you choose to hard-code your own mobile website, the standard width for a mobile website (as of 2011) is 320 pixels.

2. Limit the Use of Images

A simple banner at the top of your mobile website with your nonprofit's logo and name is a good starting point. Make sure that it links to your mobile website home page. From there, do not use images for navigation, and limit news articles to one image. Fortunately, if you are using your blog's RSS feed for mobile Web content creation, tools like MoFuse automatically shrink image sizes for faster loading and browsing. All images should be small and should be in either .jpeg or .gif format.

3. Feature Fresh Content Prominently

With the exception of mobile pages created specifically for group text messaging and QR code campaigns (donate, petitions, polls, and so on), most people will browse through only the fresh content on your mobile website. They're looking for news and campaign updates, not detailed information about your nonprofit's history, programs, mission, and values. A mobile website should not be modeled after your desktop site. The two have completely different purposes. So, make sure you feature your fresh content first (your blog feed) and calls to action after that. In time, as word gets out about your mobile website, the number of visitors will increase. Some may even bookmark it for browsing regularly. Currently, much of this browsing occurs on lunch breaks, while traveling to and from work, and while standing in line at the DMV, the grocery store, the airport, and other such places.

4. Limit Your "About Us" Content to One Page

Create one page that summarizes your "About Us" content. This is where you give shortened versions of your history, your programs, and important milestones you have achieved. You can have three or four small photos on this page to give it some color and make it more interesting, but in general, people are not interested in reading Web 1.0 content on a mobile website.

5. Link to the Mobile Versions of Your Social Networking Profiles

This is a big one! Link to the mobile versions of your Facebook Page (m.facebook.com/nonprofitorgs), your Twitter Profile (m.twitter.com/ nonprofitorgs), your YouTube Channel (m.youtube.com/nonprofit orgs), and your Flickr account (m.flickr.com/photos/nonprofitorgs). This allows your mobile visitors to like, follow, and subscribe easily, as well as browse status updates, tweets, and your most recent videos and photos. Download small social media icons and work them into the design so that they are visible on every page of your mobile web- site. Ideally, they should be featured at the top of your mobile website, since a lot of scrolling is required to view the bottom of pages on your mobile website. Also, be sure to link to your Facebook Places, Foursquare, and Gowalla pages for easy check-ins and participation.

6. Feature Group Text Alerts and E-newsletter "Subscribe" Functionality

Good online fundraisers know that you must build your lists at every opportunity. Be sure to feature the ability to subscribe to your e-newsletter and group text message campaigns on every page of your mobile website. This can either be worked into the navigation of your mobile website or added to the "Take Action" or "Get Involved" page. There are also e-newsletter and text icons available through most icon portals, like IconsPedia.com and IconDock.com, that can be placed next to your social networking icons. The number of people who regularly check their e-mail on mobile devices is rising steadily, so subscribing to an e-newsletter on a mobile website is definitely within the realm of possibility.

7. Feature a "Donate Now" Page That Is Optimized for Mobile Use

It's highly unlikely that a donor will take the time and effort to fill out a donation form that is formatted for desktop viewing. Until online giving portals offer mobile "Donate Now" pages in addition to desktop "Donate Now" pages, you will have to hard-code this page. It's likely that many vendors will begin to offer "Donate Now" pages and other tools optimized for mobile browsing in the coming years. As more become available, these will become easier and more affordable.

8. Feature "Text-to-Give Now" Functionality, if Applicable

If your nonprofit is utilizing text-to-give technology, you should include "Text-to-Give Now" mobile pages that allow donors to simply enter their phone number to make a donation. You will have to either hard-code this page yourself or use a text-to-give vendor that offers the service.

9. Feature E-advocacy Campaigns

Signing petitions and participating in e-mail action alerts on mobile websites has a bright future. Currently, they have to be hard-coded, but it's just a matter of time until services like Change.org and Care2 offer mobile optimized advocacy tools. It's also likely that new vendors specializing in mobile e-advocacy will be launched in the coming years, as well as Convio, Blackbaud, and DemocracyInAction building upon the e-advocacy services that they already offer. When these tools become available and affordable, you'll want to feature your e-advocacy campaigns on your mobile website so that people can easily "Take Action." This is a trend to monitor closely. A Canadian nonprofit called the Big Wild pioneered mobile e-advocacy through the use of a QR code. After people scanned the code, they were sent to a mobile petition to "Keep the Restigouche Watershed Wild" that could be easily signed and sent to government officials.

10. Incorporate Video into Your Mobile Website

Like all things mobile, mobile video consumption is soaring. That said, take screenshots of your best videos and incorporate them into your "About Us" or "Get Involved" page on your mobile website. They should be shrunk to 320 pixels in width and link directly to the mobile version of the video on YouTube.

11. Promote Your Mobile Website in Print Materials, on Your Website and Your Blog, and in Your Social Networking Communities

As with any other Web-based campaign, you need to promote your mobile website. Write a short blurb about your new mobile website and ask supporters to "Bookmark Your Mobile Browser!" Publish the blurb in your print newsletter, link to it on your website and on your blog, and mention it to your social networking communities. Initially, most of your mobile website traffic will come from links in text alerts and QR codes, but as mobile browsing continues to soar, much of it will come across your mobile website the old-fashioned way—through Google, Bing, Yahoo!, Opera Mini, and Safari searches conducted on smartphones.

INTRODUCTION TO QUICK RESPONSE CODES

Quick Response (QR) codes are two-dimensional bar code images that, when scanned by a camera on a smartphone (or tablet), open a link, send a text message or e-mail, or dial a phone number. You can easily create QR codes for free at sites like QRCode.kaywa.com, uQR.me, and Bit.ly. To scan a QR code, smartphone owners must first download a QR code reader (browse your app store for a "qr code reader"), then take a picture of the QR code using the camera on their smartphone. The person scanning is then either sent to a mobile Web browser to view the link inside the QR code, sent a text message or e-mail, or prompted to dial a phone number.

QR codes are ideal for location-based communications and fundraising campaigns because it is often easier to scan a QR code image than it is to open a Web browser on a smartphone and tap in a URL. Smartphones will soon be the predominant choice of cell phone subscribers, thus enabling a majority of Americans and others to scan anywhere at any time. In fact, it is likely that in the future, QR code readers will come preinstalled on all smartphones to enable a wide variety of commercial and personal transactions.

FIVE WAYS NONPROFITS CAN USE QR CODES

The most common use of QR codes in the nonprofit sector is to link to mobile Web content (donation pages, petitions and other calls to action, social networking communities, and so on), but you can also use them to send e-mails or text messages and to prompt activists to place calls to elected officials. A little creativity goes a long way in QR code campaigns. If the trend sticks, it's likely to evolve quickly and spur the launching of multiple new QR code services and tools by vendors from both the nonprofit and the business sectors, but for now, QR code campaigns are very basic and limited in functionality. It is likely to take a few years for them to go mainstream, so be sure to add a few instructional sentences on all QR code materials explaining how they work, but also be sure to always keep the destination of the QR code a mystery.

1. At Fundraising Events, Conferences, Protests, and Other Such Situations

Your nonprofit could add QR codes that link to a "Donate Now" or "Text-to-Give Now" mobile page to flyers and print materials distributed at fundraising events like annual galas and marathons. Similarly, you could add QR codes to conference materials (badges, table tents, and so on) that link to the agenda, session descriptions and speakers' bios, or polls for real-time feedback during breakout or plenary sessions. Activist organizations can use QR codes to empower rally attenders or protesters to call elected officials or sign online petitions. Again, with a little creative thinking, your nonprofit could discover countless ways to incorporate QR codes and your mobile website at events.

2. In the Community

Even with Craigslist available in cities worldwide, many communities still have bulletin boards at grocery stores, Laundromats, and restaurants and throughout college campuses where you can post flyers and promotional materials. In some ways, QR code campaigns are old school, but with a new twist. Small local nonprofits should consider posting flyers emblazoned with QR codes throughout their local community: on bulletin boards, billboards, telephone poles, car windshields, and mailboxes. For people who have never seen QR codes, this will definitely grab their attention and pique their curiosity. Also, if your nonprofit has close ties to the business community, consider launching a "Scan for Good" campaign to be posted at checkouts in retail establishments or on table tents at restaurants. Cause marketing appeals to many business owners and is likely to lead to interesting conversations while people are standing in line or sharing a meal with their family and friends.

3. In Print Newsletters, Funding Appeals, Invitations, Annual Reports, and Ads

QR codes were first used in magazine ads by the business sector. People would scan a code in an ad and then be sent to a mobile website where they could redeem a coupon, learn more information about the product, or watch a promotional video. Since then, their use has spread rapidly throughout the for-profit publishing world, and if it works there, it is likely to work for the nonprofit sector as well. For example, use them in print newsletter articles to link to videos or slideshows to make reading more interactive and visual. Put a QR code on invitations; when it is scanned, people are sent to a mobile page where they can easily RSVP. Add them to fundraising appeals with direct links to "Text-to-Give Now" pages. The possibilities are limitless.

4. On Location

QR codes are popping up everywhere—on subways, in window displays, and at airports worldwide. If your nonprofit is location-based, incorporate QR codes into your location. For example, create a QR code tour at your museum. Arts organizations could create QR code art walks. Historical societies could offer city walking tours with QR codes. Or if you are an animal shelter, use QR codes to link to a potential new pet's bio and history. Theaters can use them in playbills to link to information about cast members. Zoos, aquariums, and animal sanctuaries can use them to link to pages that discuss animal behaviors or extinction threat levels and how people can help. People are often deeply moved and inspired while they are at a museum or an animal sanctuary, and QR code campaigns allow a nonprofit to tap into that inspiration instantaneously. Not only can such campaigns be a lot of fun to create, but they can also be powerful motivators for social good.

5. On Objects

QR code readers are pretty good at what they do. You can add QR codes to T-shirts, coffee cups, pins, hats, calendars, and other such items, and most readers will get it on the first try. If your nonprofit gives such items to new members, volunteers, or conference attendees, consider adding a QR code next time around.

FINAL WORDS:
THOSE WHO DO IT FIRST, DO IT BEST

Hopefully your nonprofit is beginning to understand that the role of the social media manager is increasingly becoming much more than updating Facebook and Twitter. Good social media managers are dabbling everywhere and in everything. In fact, they are now enthusiastically evolving into social mobile media managers. Some pioneering nonprofits are even creating job descriptions for "new media managers" or "emerging media managers." Those communications and development professionals who can adapt and adopt quickly will be in high demand in the coming years. Unfortunately, many communications and staff budgets in the nonprofit sector are still being drafted like it's 2002, with a heavy focus on print and expensive, multilayered websites. Before you know it, 2015 and Mobile Web domination will be here, and by then those budgets will seem ancient and like a relic from another time. The Web moves at lightning speed now, and those that at least make an attempt to keep up will still be relevant. Those that don't will fade into the background.

Early adoption in and of itself has evolved into a powerful strategy during the rise of the Social Web. Those who do something first tend to do it best simply because they are doing it. The media, the blogosphere, the Millennials, and even Gen X are now accustomed to a rapid 24/7 cycle of news and social good. They are hungry for what's new and different. Ten years ago, early adoption of Web technology by the nonprofit sector was expensive, so that this strategy could be utilized only by large nonprofits with large budgets. Consequently, they got most of the online buzz, most of the media coverage, and the majority of donations. Today, the tools are free or low-cost. As long as your nonprofit is forward-thinking enough to understand that job descriptions, skill sets, and budgets need to shift, then you can find the time and resources to be an early adopter. To not at least try is wasting a valuable opportunity at this critical juncture and turning in Mobile Web history.

Nonprofit Examples of Excellence

- Nelson-Atkins Museum of Art: nelson-atkins.org/mobile guide
- National Public Radio: m.npr.org
- Nature Conservancy: m.nature.org
- Planned Parenthood: m.plannedparenthood.org
- World Wildlife Fund: worldwildlife.org/mobile

Google This!

- ❏ Nonprofitorgs.mobi
- ❏ Mobile seo
- ❏ Mobile web design best practices
- ❏ Wikipedia qr code
- ❏ Nonprofit qr codes
- ❏ How to: make your qr codes more beautiful
- ❏ Paperlinks.com
- ❏ Jagtag.com
- ❏ Tag.microsoft.com
- ❏ Spyderlynk.com
- ❏ 2d-code.co.uk
- ❏ Qrstuff.com

GROUP TEXT MESSAGING AND TEXT-TO-GIVE TECHNOLOGY

We have not yet incorporated mobile technology into our communications strategy, but it is very high on our list of priorities for 2012. Mobile phone use in Africa has increased fivefold over the last five years. In fact, nearly one in three people in Africa now have mobile phones, and a large number of them text on a daily basis. And that's just Africa! So, for the Global Fund, it's not a matter of if, but of when we can launch our first mobile campaign.

—*Deborah Holmes, vice president of communications, Global Fund for Women*

THE BIG PICTURE:
TEXT MESSAGING FOR GOOD

Adults in the United States now send and receive more text messages than calls on their mobile phones. For teens, text messaging trumps e-mail, social networking, and instant messaging. In fact, on average, teens in America send almost 4,000 text messages per month! Globally, the number of text messages sent annually will soon surpass 10 trillion. Compare that to the 1 trillion sent in 2008, and it's clear that text messaging is on a meteoric rise like no other tool covered in this book. Yet only a tiny fraction of those text messages come from nonprofits—at least in developed nations.

Interestingly enough, text messaging for good has been pioneered by nonprofits in Africa, Asia, and Latin America, where a cell phone and mobile Internet access is often more affordable than desktop Internet use. Quickly browsing MobileActive.org and FrontlineSMS.org clearly demonstrates that text messaging campaigns related to global health, disaster relief, and democracy were being utilized for social good in countries like Afghanistan, South Africa, Sri Lanka, Nepal, India, and Brazil long before nonprofits in the United States, Canada, Europe, and Australia used these campaigns. That's probably because of the high cost of launching and maintaining group text messaging campaigns in developed nations, but thanks to recent innovations, group text messaging is becoming more affordable for all nonprofits everywhere.

INTRODUCTION TO GROUP
TEXT MESSAGING

Until recently, text messaging, also known as Short Message Service (SMS), has mostly been used as a mode of communication between individuals on their mobile phones. Its 20-year anniversary will be 2012; the first text message was sent on a Vodafone in 1992 from one text messaging pioneer to another and simply said, "Merry

Christmas." Since then, trillions of text messages have been sent, and with recent innovations in group text messaging, sometimes also referred to as broadcast text messaging, the number of text messages sent and received annually is set to grow exponentially at a rate that is difficult to even conceptualize mathematically.

Group text messaging enables nonprofits, institutions of higher education, and businesses to send text messages to large numbers of subscribers en masse. In the nonprofit sector, group text messaging has been used primarily to send urgent news updates and calls to action, to remind supporters to donate, and to broadcast volunteer opportunities. That said, the vast majority of nonprofits haven't even considered incorporating group text messaging into their communications and fundraising campaigns, or if they did consider it, they were unable to use it because it has been highly cost-prohibitive to become an early adopter. However, that is no longer the case. A number of new group text messaging services have come to market in recent years, increasing competition and thus lowering the fees associated with launching and maintaining group text alert campaigns. Most nonprofits can now at least experiment with group text messaging and start building their mobile lists.

SELECTING A GROUP TEXTING VENDOR

To receive group text messages, people must subscribe by sending a keyword to a short code (a five- or six-digit phone number). Keywords and short codes are also used to empower text-to-give campaigns, such as, "Text SEIU to 787753 to subscribe to receive text alerts!" Once people send the keyword to the short code, they are sent a text asking them to reply "Yes" or "Y" to confirm that they want to receive the group text messages. People can unsubscribe at any time by replying "STOP" to any given text message. To send group text messages, your nonprofit must first sign up with a group text messaging vendor and purchase a keyword. Group text messages can then be sent easily from a Web-based dashboard offered by the vendor. Fees vary widely from vendor to vendor, and, unfortunately, the vendors that specifically serve the nonprofit sector have been the most expensive and usually require contracts. In time that's likely to change, so before you select a vendor, do your research and compare your options carefully.

- *Mobile Commons, mGive, and MobileCause.* Mobile Commons and mGive pioneered mobile technology for nonprofits. Both offer a suite of tools ranging from group text messaging to text-to-give functionality. They have also traditionally been the most expensive. If you can afford them, their tool sets are phenomenal. MobileCause is another vendor that serves the nonprofit sector, but is a little less expensive. Again, over time, these services are probably going to become more affordable, so monitor and compare their fees and exercise caution when signing a contract for a period longer than six months. That said, these vendors understand the needs of the nonprofit sector and have created mobile advocacy tools, Facebook apps, and widgets that are very useful to nonprofits and are not provided by vendors that serve the business sector. If it makes financial sense, using one of these three vendors for your mobile technology campaigns is a wise decision. That said, these vendors serve only nonprofits in the United States. For nonprofits in the U.K., InstaGiv provides group text messaging and text-to-give services, and for nonprofits in Canada, there is ZipGive. In all other countries, mobile communications and fundraising are still in their infancy stages or not yet available.

- *Ez Texting, Group Texting, and TextMarks.* What these vendors lack in bells and whistles, they make up for in simplicity of use and low fees. Their primary focus is on offering group text messaging and a dashboard that makes it easy to manage messages and contacts. Again, fees vary from service to service, but with fees starting at $25 to $50 a month, these services make experimenting and mobile list building and management possible for many nonprofits.

- *FrontlineSMS*. FrontlineSMS is a free, open-source software program that enables users to send group text messages from computers or mobile phones. It must be downloaded and is available only to nonprofit organizations. Used widely throughout the globe, FrontlineSMS has empowered a texting revolution at the grassroots by nonprofits in developing nations and has become a beacon for social good in mobile technology. FrontlineSMS requires that you have a GSM modem or a mobile phone connected to your computer via Serial, USB, or Bluetooth, and some initial tech know-how is needed to set up the software, but sending group text messages is free.

ELEVEN GROUP TEXT MESSAGING BEST PRACTICES FOR NONPROFITS

The nonprofit sector is new to group text messaging, and because of that, most best practices have yet to be determined. There are some basic guidelines to follow when you are launching and managing your group text campaigns; in the beginning, however, your number one objective should be to begin building your mobile list. It is illegal to buy, sell, or trade mobile phone numbers, unlike e-mail and snail mail addresses. As a result, it takes time to build a list, so the sooner you start, the better. The open rate of text messages is over 90 percent, since those who sign up tend to be your most committed supporters, so making the effort to promote your group texting campaign(s) and build your mobile list now could prove to be extremely valuable in years to come as the popularity of group text messaging continues to skyrocket. That said, the purpose of your group texting campaigns will evolve over time as the technology develops, but initially it's best to approach group text messaging with the idea of alerting your subscribers to important breaking news that is relevant to your nonprofit's mission and programs, and as a means of sending your subscribers occasional reminders about getting more involved in your nonprofit's work.

1. Add a "Subscribe to Receive Text Alerts!" Pitch to Your Website, E-newsletter, Blog, and Print Materials

Create a "Subscribe to Receive Text Alerts!" page on your website that details the purpose of your group texting campaign, how it works, how often text messages will be sent, and, most important, how to subscribe. In addition to information on subscribing by keyword and short code, you should also embed an online form or widget (provided by your vendor) on the page that easily allows people to type in their mobile number to subscribe instantaneously. This new page should then be linked near the e-newsletter subscribe option on your website and blog. You should also add a "Mobile" field to your donation forms and event sign-up sheets, and add your keyword and short code subscription information to your print newsletters. It's also crucial to add a link to your "Subscribe to Receive Text Alerts!" page in your e-newsletter (80 percent of new group text subscribers come from e-mail lists!) and your "Thank You" landing pages and e-mails. Finally, there are icons for "SMS" that you can download and integrate with your social networking icons on your website and your blog. Of course, you also want to create a "Subscribe to Receive Text Alerts!" page on your mobile website.

2. Create a "Text-to-Subscribe" Graphic for Social Networking Sites

You should create a graphic that visually compels people to subscribe to your text alerts. Whether it is a custom graphic designed in Photoshop or simply your text-to-subscribe keyword and short code pitch (for example, "Text PETA to 73822 to subscribe to receive text alerts!") embedded in a powerful photo, you want an image that you can upload to send out in Facebook status updates, link to in tweets, upload to Flickr, and so on. Simple text pitches aren't enough to compel people to subscribe. Get creative in integrating your text-to-subscribe keyword and short code pitch into photos, slideshows, or even your YouTube Channel banner. Additionally, you should also occasionally link to your "Subscribe to Receive Text Alerts!" page in status updates and tweets.

3. Pitch Your Keyword and Short Code in Check-Ins

When you are checking in to places, venues, and spots on location-based communities, add your text-to-subscribe keyword and short code pitch to status updates and shouts. Your friends on location-based communities will literally have their smartphone in their hands as they read your status updates and shouts, making it much more likely that they will subscribe to your group text messaging campaign.

4. Add Your Text-to-Subscribe Keyword and Short Code Pitch to Your Twitter Background

If your nonprofit has the ability to create custom backgrounds for your Twitter Profile, it's smart to add a text-to-subscribe keyword and short code pitch. Even though Twitter backgrounds are simple images that cannot include hyperlinks to other websites, nonprofits often do add their website and social networking URLs to Twitter backgrounds. If Twitterers are willing to open a new browser and manually type in URLs, then they are just as likely to pick up their phone and send a text to subscribe.

5. Send Text Messages That Are Timely and Relevant to Current Events

Most often, your group text messages should be relevant to current events or important news updates about your nonprofit. They should be timely, should often communicate a sense of urgency, and, when possible, should include a call to action. Group text messaging is primarily meant to mobilize your supporters instantaneously wherever they are located. For this reason, group text messaging is especially relevant to advocacy and activist organizations.

6. Send a Mixture of Informational and Call-to-Action Text Messages

You should occasionally send simple informational group text messages that are not necessarily timely, but are useful or inspirational. Ideas include a powerful quote or statistic, health tips, shopping suggestions, and "Save the Date!" event announcements. A mixture of text message content is good; however, before you send out a text message, always ask yourself whether the message is useful. If it is not, don't send it! Since the open rate for text messaging is so high, each and every one of your messages should be well thought out and interesting.

7. Send Periodic Text Message Reminders to Donate Online or via Text-to-Give

It's also wise to send group text messages reminding people to donate on your website or to text-to-give, especially at the end of the year, when most donations are made. It's likely that in years to come, tens of thousands of nonprofits will be sending text message donation reminders en masse on December 30, so now, before the law of diminishing returns begins to kick in, is a very good time to be an early adopter.

8. Don't Send More than Two or Three Text Messages per Month

Open, click-through, and unsubscribe rates will clearly guide the frequency of your group text messaging campaigns, but at the beginning, limit your text messages to two or three a month maximum. Subscribers are much more likely to pay attention to your text messages and take action if they are sent infrequently. It's very easy to unsubscribe from group text messaging campaigns, so proceed with patience. If you are to retain your subscribers, your text messages have to be good. Most subscribers hear their smartphones chime when your message arrives. If they stop what they are doing, pick up their phone, and see a mediocre text message from your nonprofit, they will reply with "STOP" in two seconds flat.

9. Link to Your Mobile Website in Text Messages!

Your subscribers will be reading your text messages on their mobile phones, not their desktops or laptops. Therefore, do not link to your desktop site in text messages! That said, not everyone will be able to view your links on their phones, but smartphones and data plans will continue to fall in price in the coming years, ensuring the continued rise of Mobile Web browsing.

10. Pitch Your Social Networking Communities in Text Messages

Every few months, send out a text message letting people know that your nonprofit has a presence on Facebook, Twitter, YouTube, Foursquare, and other such sites. Ideally, you should link to one Web page optimized for mobile browsing that includes links to all your communities in their mobile format, or to the home page of your mobile website if you have social networking icons featured prominently. Otherwise, mention your communities individually in text messages strategically spaced out during the year.

11. Use Bit.ly to Track Click-Through Rates

The more expensive group text messaging vendors offer useful stats and tracking tools, but if you want to save money and opt for one of the low-cost vendors, then you can use Bit.ly to track click-through rates in text messages. Shrinking the links also allows you more characters in your text messages. It's wise to create a separate Bit.ly account for mobile tracking only. It makes it easier to track your mobile progress over time if your Bit.ly links are not merged with your desktop click-throughs and traffic.

INTRODUCTION TO TEXT-TO-GIVE TECHNOLOGY

The use of text-to-give technology reached a fever pitch in the weeks and months immediately following the tragic earthquake in Haiti in January 2010. The American Red Cross alone raised more than $30 million. Text-to-give thus proved itself to be very effective in raising funds for disaster relief, especially when you have news media and celebrities broadcasting your text-to-give keyword and short code pitch to millions of people. Unfortunately, most nonprofits do not have those kinds of connections, and the majority of nonprofits that have experimented with text-to-give campaigns thus far have been disappointed with the results. Some location-based nonprofits like museums, zoos, and aquariums have had success with text-to-give campaigns because they have the ability to inspire people to give instantaneously while on location, but for the most part, unless your nonprofit can tap into media connections, celebrity power, or large events (concerts, sporting events, and so on), the dollars raised through text-to-give technology are likely to be minimal.

Utilizing text-to-give technology is expensive, and until it becomes more affordable, your nonprofit shouldn't even consider experimenting with it unless you think you can inspire 100 donors a month to donate at least $5 each. If your nonprofit has those resources available, mGive, Mobile Commons, and MobileCause all offer text-to-give technology. In cooperation with the Mobile Giving Foundation (mobilegiving.org), they will set you up with a unique keyword and short code to empower your text-to-give campaign, such as "Text PANDA to 90999 to donate $10 to the San Diego Zoo!" Most vendors require start-up fees, a contract, and a monthly rate ranging from \$150 to \$500, but as with group text messaging technology, as more vendors flood the market, prices are dropping rapidly and significantly. Definitely do some comparison shopping!

FIVE WAYS TO PROMOTE YOUR TEXT-TO-GIVE CAMPAIGNS

One of the reasons why text-to-give fundraising has been a struggle for most nonprofits could be that very few resources on how to promote a text-to-give campaign successfully have been available to nonprofits. Simply giving your text-to-give keyword and short code pitch in print materials, tweets, and status updates isn't enough to inspire your donors to grab their mobile phones and make a donation. A little more creativity and graphic design work is required. First on your list should be to create at least five powerful visuals with your text-to-give pitch. They can be photos that speak to your nonprofit's work or custom graphics created entirely in Photoshop. Either way, you need to be able to pitch your text-to-give campaigns online in a way that is visually compelling and inspirational. You probably already have at least five powerful photos, so open them in Photoshop or upload them to Picnik.com, and simply add your text-to-give pitch along the bottom of the images.

1. To Your Social Networking Communities

Once you have the images created, then upload them to your Facebook Page and send them out periodically in status updates. You can also upload the images to Flickr and then link to them in tweets. Additionally, if you have been approved for the YouTube Nonprofit Program, add text overlays to your videos with a text-to-give pitch. Post the videos on Facebook and Twitter as well. As with all donation tools, if text-to-give pitches are to be successful, you have to integrate them into all your communications.

2. On your Desktop Website, Blog, E-newsletter, and Mobile Website

Next, embed a simple, well-designed graphic or photo with your text-to-give pitch on your website, your blog, and your mobile website. Underneath the image, include "Text-to-Give Now!" language that links to a page on your desktop and mobile websites where supporters can easily enter their mobile number to make a donation. Once they enter their number, they are automatically sent a text message asking them to confirm their donation. Your text-to-give vendor should provide you with the code that enables Web-based text donations. Of course, you should also promote your text-to-give campaigns in your e-newsletter.

3. In Group Text Messages

A text message with your text-to-give pitch that links to a "Text-to-Give Now!" page on your mobile website is smart. Think about it. Your subscribers already have their smartphones in their hands and do not need to enter a name, address, or credit card number to make a donation. This is probably one of the biggest reasons why most donors haven't embraced text-to-give technology—the vast majority of nonprofits that are experimenting with text-to-give fundraising do not have mobile websites or group text messaging campaigns!

4. On Location-Based Communities

Shout out your text-to-give pitch during check-ins. Take pictures of your text-to-give images with your smartphone and upload them to places, venues, and spots when you are checking in. Mention your text-to-give pitch and link to it in tips and to dos. Again, most people are already going to have their smartphone in their hand when they see your pitch on a location-based community, thus making it much more likely that they will text-to-give to your nonprofit, especially if your nonprofit is regularly active on those communities.

5. In Print Materials

Finally, be sure to incorporate an inspirational image or graphic with your text-to-give pitch in your print newsletter, fundraising appeals, reports, magazines, and promotional brochures. Many people also enjoy reading print materials on the go, making it much more likely that they have their mobile phone nearby.

FINAL WORDS:
THE FUTURE OF FUNDRAISING IS MOBILE

As in the early years of Donate Now technology, most donors will need time to get accustomed to giving through their mobile phones and trusting the technology. Even so, the future of mobile giving may not be through text-to-give technology as it functions today. Many donors don't like their donations showing up on their mobile phone bills. We could eventually be donating through mobile giving portals or smartphone apps using our mobile numbers, credit cards, or mobile wallets. It's too early to tell. Mobile giving will be innovating and evolving constantly for years to come. However, mobile devices will be the dominant technology used to access the Internet worldwide by 2015. Exactly how we will raise funds and give on the Mobile Web is yet to be seen, but there is no denying that the future of fundraising is in mobile technology.

Nonprofit Examples of Excellence: Text-to-Give

- American Red Cross
- Clinton Bush Haiti Fund
- Keep a Child Alive
- St. Jude's Children's Research Hospital
- The Trevor Project

Nonprofit Examples of Excellence: Group Text Messaging

- American Society for the Prevention of Cruelty to Animals (ASPCA)

- DoSomething.org

- Service Employees International Union (SEIU)

- TeenSource.org

- Text4Baby.org

Google This!

- ❑ Wikipedia text messaging

- ❑ Texting pew internet

- ❑ Nonprofit text messaging benchmarks study m + r

- ❑ Enonprofit benchmarks study m + r

- ❑ Text messages stats

- ❑ Nonprofit text messaging campaigns

- ❑ Nonprofit text-to-give campaigns

- ❑ Five ways to promote your text-to-give campaigns on social media

- ❑ Text-to-give case studies

- ❑ @nonprofitorgs mobile flickr

- ❑ Mobile wallets

- ❑ Jumio.com

SMARTPHONE APPS

Creating a women's safety app has been one of the most rewarding and challenging undertakings. A surprising discovery in the process was the intensity of app promotion required and the money that it costs to do it effectively. For an app to truly go viral, it takes a lot more than mass downloads; it really requires mass marketing. But we knew from the outset that if we wanted to reach young women about safety, then we needed to reach them where they live—on their phones. For us, the investment was worth it.

—Corinne Rusch-Drutz, director of communications & membership development, YWCA Canada

THE BIG PICTURE: AN APP ECONOMY FOR NONPROFITS?

The Apple App Store opened on iTunes in July of 2008 with 500 apps for the iPhone and the iPod Touch available for download, of which 25 percent were free. Two months later, there were 3,000 apps available and more than 55,000,000 downloads had taken place, giving rise to a new era in our tech economy based on building, buying, and downloading apps for smartphones and tablets. By the end of 2010, annual revenues from app stores for Apple, Android, RIM for BlackBerry, Nokia, and Samsung had totaled more than $5 billion, and according to a report by Gartner released early in 2010, the app economy is on track to surpass $15 billion in annual revenues in 2011 and total downloads of almost 18 billion since the opening of the Apple App Store in 2008.

And that is just beginning. Now that smartphones and tablets are becoming mainstream, Gartner goes on to predict that by the end of 2014, downloads will total more than 185 billion, with close to 80 percent of those downloads being free. The proliferation of smartphone and tablet apps in the coming years will no doubt be mind-boggling to many. The question is, where do nonprofits and social good fit into this new app economy? Many nonprofits have launched apps in the past, but most of those apps have not been successful in terms of download numbers and consistent use. The brutal reality of the app economy is that 26 percent of apps are opened only once, and after an initial downloading-of-apps spree, most smartphone and tablet owners tend to use only 10 or 15 apps regularly—those that they find most useful in their daily lives. Most apps, nonprofit or not, simply do not maintain a user's interest.

For many nonprofits, the rise of the app economy was a time of excitement and possibility. In 2008 and 2009, many nonprofits, equipped with shiny new iPhones, were convinced that apps were the Next Big Thing in nonprofit communications and fundraising. Though the impulse to be an early adopter was a good one, these nonprofits may have been a little too far ahead of the curve. Or, they may just have been wrong. It's too early to tell. Mobile technology and how the online commons use it to access the Mobile Web is constantly in flux. It's yet to be seen whether nonprofits need smartphone and tablet apps in addition to a mobile website. Much of that decision will depend on the nonprofit's mission and programs. Not every nonprofit (in fact, not even most) needs a smartphone or tablet app.

FIVE MUST-HAVE CHARACTERISTICS OF A NONPROFIT SMARTPHONE APP

If your nonprofit is going to launch a smartphone app, then you need to be aware from the beginning that you will probably need to launch and maintain a minimum of two, possibly three versions of the app (for the Android, iPhone/iPod Touch, and BlackBerry) in order to be compatible with the smartphones used by the majority of consumers. When many nonprofits were launching iPhone/iPod Touch apps in 2009, they just didn't see it coming that Android would surpass the iPhone (and BlackBerry). Many spent tens of thousands of dollars on apps that now have a relatively small market share, and for that reason alone, many nonprofits are beginning to understand that mobile websites as the entry point for the Mobile Web often make more sense. That said, the app economy is on the brink of exploding, and there could be a solid future in building and launching a suite of smartphone apps for your nonprofit, but only if they are built with the five characteristics given here placed high on your priority list.

1. It Must Be Useful

Odds are that your supporters don't want to download your app just to read your blog and learn about your mission, vision, and programs. Your app needs to have a utilitarian purpose. The most successful apps are those related to breaking news and games, and those that accentuate daily life (health, relationships, horoscopes, literature, film, TV, and so on). In the nonprofit sector, apps that provide breaking news, volunteer opportunities, information about conscious consumerism, health or living tips, the ability to sign petitions and participate in e-mail or mobile action alerts, and other such things could have great appeal to the smartphone masses. That said, unless your app is very useful and exceptionally well developed, don't expect people to pay to download it. The concept of downloading apps as a way of giving to charity thus far has not produced results for most nonprofits.

2. It Looks Good

Many of the do-it-yourself app builders, like AppMakr or SwebApps, make it incredibly easy and cost-effective to launch your own smartphone app, but their design tools and functionality are limited. If your nonprofit is known for providing regular breaking news, then these tools are a great option for building and launching a simple app meant solely to broadcast news. However, if your nonprofit is serious about launching a suite of apps that goes beyond sharing news, yet will still be useful and unique in its concept, then you will probably need to hire an app developer and designer. Fees range wildly depending upon the depth of the app, but for top-notch development, a minimum budget of $10,000 is required. In terms of aesthetics, app design is currently based on using bold colors, thin sans-serif fonts, exceptionally well-designed graphics, and professional photography.

3. It Is Bug-Free

Smartphone users have almost zero tolerance for apps that crash, freeze, or don't work on the first or second try. Test your apps frequently throughout the creation and launch process to check for bugs and other issues. After you submit your app to the app stores, you should also review subsequent upgrades for tech glitches and bugs. Users can rate and review your app inside the app stores, so make sure that the first version and every subsequent version are as solid as possible, or people will never open your app again.

4. It Links to a Mobile Website(s)

It's shocking how many smartphone apps link to desktop sites! There has been a gargantuan disconnect, and many developers have turned a blind eye to the fact that it makes absolutely no sense for a smartphone app to link to a desktop site, especially "Donate Now" pages. Thankfully, throughout 2011, the "Aha!" moments about mobile pages grew in number and volume, but it's been a long three years of tapping uselessly on desktop links inside of smartphone apps.

5. It Does Not Require Immediate Registration to Use

Nonprofit fundraisers know the importance of building e-newsletter and group text messaging campaign lists, but asking for an e-mail address or mobile number at first tap is overkill. If a user is required to give you his contact information before he even gets to see what your app looks like and what it does, you've lost him.

LAUNCHING AND MAINTAINING A SMARTPHONE APP

When one considers that smartphone downloads have not yet even come close to reaching their peak, and that they are predicted to increase dramatically in the years to come, it's clear that we are still in the early adoption phase, especially in the nonprofit sector. As this book has reiterated many times, early adoption itself can be a successful communications strategy. However, unless you think that you can create an exceptionally useful, well-designed app that will pay for itself in either brand equity or download fees, err on the side of caution and frugality. If your nonprofit wants to launch a smartphone app, then you have two options.

1. Do It Yourself Using a Vendor like AppMakr or SwebApps

The cost of tools like these ranges from $10 to $25 a month for app hosting and customer support. They offer the ability to easily create simple apps for the Android and iPhone and iPod Touch (not BlackBerry), and increasingly for the Windows Phone and tablets, through a Web-based dashboard. While these are basic, upgrades in functionality and improvements to the tool sets occur regularly. Such vendors also work with you throughout the process of submitting your apps to the app stores. Your biggest expense will be hiring a graphic designer for your app's buttons and interface. For those nonprofits that want to be early adopters and are not fixated on large download numbers, these tools enable almost any nonprofit to launch smartphone apps.

2. Hire a Developer

Again, fees vary widely—from $10,000 to $50,000. However, as with all new technologies, the prices will get lower over time as new tools and developers flood the market. In the early days of Web 1.0, website designers were charging the same fees that app developers are charging today. If you are presented with a price quote in the $10,000 to $50,000 range, be sure that the idea behind the app is exceptional and that the developer has a proven track record of success and experience. To begin your research into hiring a developer that specifically serves the nonprofit sector, start with Free Range Studios (freerange.com) and EchoDitto (echoditto.com).

FIVE WAYS TO PROMOTE YOUR SMARTPHONE APP

One of the biggest perks of being an early adopter of smartphone apps is the "wow factor." Even if all your nonprofit can afford to launch is a simple, do-it-yourself app, you still reap the benefits of being able to announce to your supporters that you have a new iPhone and/or Android app available for download. That said, no matter how great your app is, if you're not promoting it correctly, it won't get downloaded. There will soon be more than one million apps available for download in app stores, and if smartphone users are to be made aware of yours, you are going to have to promote it heavily.

1. On Your Desktop Website, Blog, E-newsletter, and Mobile Website

To begin, create a "Download Now" page on your desktop and mobile websites that includes a screenshot of your app, a bullet list of its top features, and a direct download link to your app(s) in the app stores. For your blog, design a graphic and insert it in the promotional column linking directly to the desktop's "Download Now" page. Simply having a graphic on your desktop and mobile websites that links directly to the app(s) in the app stores is not enough! You must have a "Download Now" page with your nonprofit's branding to better pitch your app(s). Also, your "Download Now" graphic with a link to your "Download Now" mobile page should be featured prominently throughout your mobile website, since visitors will already have their smartphones in hand, thus significantly increasing the likelihood that they will download your app. Finally, of course, announce and link to your "Download Now" page in your e-newsletter and on the home page of your desktop website. It would also be wise to incorporate share functionality on this page so that your supporters can easily help spread the word online about your app(s).

2. To Your Social Networking Communities

Promote your app(s) by linking to your "Download Now" page in tweets two or three times a month, post it with a status update on Facebook, and incorporate your "Download Now" pitch into your LinkedIn Group templates and Company Page. This is simple enough and obvious, yet most nonprofits with smartphone apps have not created "Download Now" pages on their websites!

3. In Group Text Messages

Be sure to let your subscribers know that they can easily download your app with a couple of taps by linking to your "Download Now" mobile page in group text messages. The fact that so few nonprofits launched group text messaging campaigns and mobile websites in 2008, 2009, and 2010 may be one reason why the overall download rate of nonprofit smartphone apps is low. That could change dramatically in the coming years as nonprofits get better at utilizing mobile technology and promoting their mobile campaigns.

4. On Location-Based Communities

Many places, venue, and spot pages allow links to be posted—if not directly, then through tips or notes. Again, when most users will be viewing your nonprofit's places, venue, or spot page is going to be while they are checking in using their smartphones, thus significantly increasing the likelihood that they will tap to download your app on location-based communities.

5. In Print Materials

Although this is probably the least effective in terms of downloads (but high in wow factor, however), be sure to promote your new app(s) in your print newsletter, annual report, brochures, and other such material.

WHAT ABOUT TABLET APPS?

There's no doubt that the use of tablets is skyrocketing and has surpassed even the most generous of analysts' predictions. The first tablet, the iPad, was launched by Apple in April 2010, and by the end of the year, it had sold more than 15 million units, triple what most analysts expected, including Apple's. Since then, Dell, Google, HP, and many others have launched their own tablets. Conservative estimates by Forrester Research indicate that by the end of 2015, there will be 81 million tablet users in the United States alone.

As tablet technology expands and evolves, many nonprofit professionals are likely to be using tablets regularly for work. They will become an integral tool for the nonprofit sector in the years to come, but does your nonprofit need to launch a tablet app? Probably not, at least not right away. First, you can convert many smartphone apps to tablet apps through a process called porting, which essentially tweaks the software and reconfigures images for tablet use. That said, most iPhone and iPod Touch apps already work on the iPad, so porting is not usually necessary for Apple tablet apps, and that is also likely to be the case in the future for Android apps as well. Second, because tablet screens are bigger than smartphone screens, and as smartphone data speeds become faster, you will be allowed more creativity to design and build a mobile website for your nonprofit that can be easily viewed on all smartphones and optimized for tablet use, thus eliminating the need for smartphone and tablet apps—maybe. Third, building a tablet app from scratch is expensive, and again, unless it is incredibly useful and has a significant wow factor, there's no need to rush into building a tablet app. It's also likely that you will have to launch and maintain multiple versions of your tablet app as the tablet market diversifies. That said, if your nonprofit is related to breaking news (NPR), publishes a magazine (National Geographic) or books (National Audubon Society), or offers tours and guides (Museum of Modern Art), then launching a tablet app should be placed on your to-do list for 2012 or 2013—maybe. We have to wait and see how the mobile app vs. the mobile website debate plays itself out.

FINAL WORDS:
BEWARE OF EXPENSIVE,
SHINY NEW TOOLS!

Many nonprofits rushed to launch an iPhone app in the year or two after the release of the iPhone in 2007. Madly in love with their shiny new tool, they spent tens of thousands of dollars building, launching, and maintaining an iPhone app that by the beginning of 2011 was not compatible with the majority of the smartphones that were in use. Many people simply could not afford an iPhone and AT&T's data plans in those early years, and when the less expensive Android operating system was made available in late 2008, new consumers increasingly chose the more cost-effective smartphone throughout 2009 and 2010, so much so that Android became the number one smartphone worldwide by January 2011.

That said, this begs the question and should inspire debate about class, race, and gender and how they affect the app economy. Especially in the early days, iPhone users were more often white, male, college-educated, and from the middle and upper classes. As the voice and conscience of social good on the Mobile Web, nonprofits must always ruminate and research demographics in emerging technologies before rushing in to adopt the next shiny new tool. The good news is that as all smartphones, tablets, and data plans become less expensive and more accessible, the barriers of class and race on the Mobile Web will crumble. In the meantime, be wise and beware of expensive, shiny new tools!

Nonprofit Examples of Excellence: Smartphone Apps

- American Hiking Society: HIKE

- Monterey Bay Aquarium: Seafood Watch

- People for the Ethical Treatment of Animals: PETA

- VolunteerMatch: VolunteerMatch

- YWCA Canada: Safety Siren

Nonprofit Examples of Excellence: Tablet Apps

- Alliance for Climate Protection: Our Choice

- Museum of Modern Art: MoMA

- National Audubon Society: A Field Guide to North American Birds

- National Geographic: National Geographic Interactive

- Public Broadcasting System: PBS

Google This!

- ❏ Build your own iphone app

- ❏ Build your own android app

- ❏ Build your own tablet app

- ❏ Red nose day iphone app

- ❑ Sierra club eco hero iphone app

- ❑ Wateraid toiletfinder for uk iphone app

- ❑ App stores

- ❑ Top 10 reviews mobile phone service providers

- ❑ How to: optimize your website for tablets

- ❑ How to: create mobile advertising campaigns for your nonprofit

- ❑ Urban airship push notifications

- ❑ Mobile web digital divide

CONCLUSION: WHAT'S NEXT?

In 1996, at the age of 24, I did my first search on the Internet through Yahoo.com. A friend sat me down and said, "You have to see this amazing Yahoo! thing." With bated breath, we typed in the word *diosa* and clicked "Search." On dial-up, and thus about 45 seconds later, Yahoo! pulled up thousands of results with the word *diosa*. This was at a time when first-draft research papers were written by hand or on typewriters, information was accessible only in libraries and books, and correspondence was done through the postal service. I was fresh from a study abroad trip where I had studied ancient Diosas Mayas in the Yucatán Peninsula, and this seemingly instantaneous result of thousands of diosas had me awed and enamored with the Internet from that very first click. Soon thereafter, I signed up for my first "electronic mail" account on Yahoo!. That first year of using and experimenting with the Internet and e-mail was life-changing. It felt as if I had been born at one of the greatest times in world history. I was of a generation that witnessed and experienced the birth of the Internet on a mass scale.

And that was only 15 years ago. Since then, we've gone through the rise of content management systems for websites, do-it-yourself mass e-mail communications, online activism and fundraising, blogging, and social networking. And today, for the Mobile Web and every new tool and possibility that comes with it, it's like it's 1996 all over again. When I ponder where we could be 50 years from now, or even 15, what the Internet will be is beyond anything that most of us can conceptualize except in the realm of science fiction. The use of the Internet as a tool to create social good has only just begun, and, as many of us hoped and dreamed in the late 1990s, it is making the world a better place.

That said, using the Internet for social good is by no means easy, and sometimes it's even ugly. Often you must expose the nefariousness of corrupt governments and human greed before you can challenge and change it, and sometimes that can feel like a heavy burden to bear—and, as always, nonprofits are the first to rise to such a challenge. Every tweet and status update shared on the Social Web by nonprofit professionals, activists, and do-gooders is one more contribution to the Greater Good. Collectively, we're using the Internet to contribute to a future that will (hopefully) be better for all human beings, animals, and our planet.

However, now, in my sixth year on the Social Web, I am beginning to clearly understand that social media is only the beginning of the story of *how the Internet saved the world*. It's a necessary evolution in Web communications to get us connected and empowered so that we can act when things really start to get tough: extreme global poverty and disease, mass extinction of species, water and food shortages, overpopulation, climate change, and the further destruction of our natural resources. Social media has made me more aware of the problems that we face, and, consequently, I have never been more inspired to foster social good and take action. The same is true of millions of others all over the world. Social media has awakened many people from their blissful slumbers of ignorance and catalyzed them into action.

The Static Web taught us how to broadcast our mission and our message to the masses. The Social Web empowered us to connect, share, and inspire. Combined, the two are a powerful force for social good. Today, we're on the brink of another evolution in the Web that is built upon and complementary to the two eras that came before it. The Web will soon be accessible anywhere, at any time. It will be mobile. As long as we don't become complacent—if we stay strong, remain focused even though bad news is swirling all around us, and stand firm and educate ourselves to keep the Internet of the People and for the People—then the power of the Web over the next 20 years could help prevent immense suffering and tragic loss. I have no idea what the new tools we will use will look like, how they will function, or what they will enable us to do, but I do know that none of them will work without you. Your passion. Your conviction. Your dedication. More than ever, the world needs you to fight the good fight.

As far as what's next, I envision social media becoming more deeply ingrained in our daily lives and Internet TV transforming our world and our living rooms. A rise in mobile advocacy, activism, and philanthropy is inevitable. But beyond that, the only things I am certain of are that technology is never going to move backward and that it is evolving faster than most nonprofit communicators and fundraisers ever imagined. The good news is that an incredibly resourceful, socially aware, tech-savvy generation of new nonprofit professionals and activists that grew up during the rise of the Social Web and mobile technology is coming of age. When their expertise is combined with the knowledge and experience of the nonprofit Web pioneers that came before them, and if we commit to working together and empowering our friends, followers, and fans to join us, then we are well prepared to transform our social ills into a triumph for social good.

YOUR NONPROFIT TECH CHECKLIST

GETTING STARTED: ORGANIZATION AND PLANNING

❑ Subscribe to, like, and follow large organizations with a mission that is similar to yours.

❑ Subscribe to social media and mobile technology blogs.

❑ Define your goals and objectives.

❑ Get the necessary training (HTML, digital photography, video, social media, and mobile technology).

❑ Create a master login sheet and reserve vanity URLs.

❑ Define metrics of measurement and create a social media ROI spreadsheet.

❑ Create a Google account.

❑ Sign up for Google Alerts.

❑ Experiment with social media dashboards.

❑ Write social media and mobile technology policies.

❑ Hire a graphic designer to design a square avatar(s).

❑ Purchase a smartphone and/or tablet.

❑ Purchase a digital camera.

❑ Purchase a pocket camcorder.

❏ Create an e-mail signature that includes your website, blog, and social networking URLs.

❏ Visit nonprofitorgsblog.org to review a list of crucial updates to *Social Media for Social Good* since its publication date.

WEB 1.0: THE STATIC WEB

1. Website

❏ Purchase .org domain name for website and e-mail addresses.

❏ Purchase a website hosting package.

❏ Select a website vendor.

❏ Write content and secure photos for website pages.

❏ Hire a graphic designer to prepare website banner(s) and custom graphics.

❏ Add e-newsletter and text alert subscribe functionality.

❏ Add "Donate Now" button to your home page.

❏ Add social networking icons.

2. E-newsletter

❏ Select an e-newsletter vendor.

❏ Design an e-newsletter template.

❏ Add e-newsletter subscribe functionality to your blog.

❏ Add e-newsletter subscribe functionality to your social networking communities.

❏ Add e-newsletter subscribe functionality to your mobile website.

❏ Add a website, blog, and social networking pitch to your "Thank You for Subscribing" e-mail.

❏ Add a website, blog, and social networking pitch to your "Thank You for Subscribing" landing page.

3. "Donate Now" Fundraising

❏ Select a Donate Now vendor.

❏ Create a "Donate Now" landing page with your nonprofit's branding inside of your website.

❏ Add charity ratings graphics to your "Donate Now" landing page, if applicable.

❏ Add a "Donate Now" button to every page of your website.

❏ Add a social networking pitch to your "Thanks for Your Donation" landing page.

❏ Add a video or slideshow to your "Thank You" landing page, if applicable.

❏ Add a social networking pitch to your "Thanks for Your Donation" e-mail.

❏ Launch a sustainer program, if applicable.

❏ Launch a gift donation program, if applicable.

❏ Launch a peer-to-peer fundraising campaign, if applicable.

WEB 2.0: THE SOCIAL WEB

1. Facebook

❏ Create a Facebook Page.

❏ Design custom tabs.

❏ Find your Facebook voice.

❏ Find and monitor your Facebook Community Page, if applicable.

❏ Claim your Facebook Places Page, if applicable.

2. Twitter

❏ Create a Twitter Profile.

❏ Design a custom background.

❏ Find your Twitter voice.

❏ Create Twitter lists.

❏ Create an account on Bit.ly.

❏ Create an account on Twtpoll.com.

❏ Create an account on TwitPic, TwitVid, or yfrog, if applicable.

❏ Create a Twibbon for your nonprofit.

❏ Experiment with HootSuite (or TweetDeck).

❏ Experiment with Twitter social good apps and portals.

❏ Launch a Twitter fundraising campaign, if applicable.

3. YouTube

❏ Create a YouTube Channel.

❏ Design your YouTube Channel.

❏ Create and upload videos.

❏ Subscribe to funders and partners.

❏ Friend local media and supporters.

❏ Create an Animoto.com account and apply to Animoto for a Cause.

❏ Apply to the YouTube Nonprofit Program.

❑ Design a custom banner, sidebar column image, and video page banner, if applicable.

❑ Create a "Thank You" video, if applicable.

4. Flickr

❑ Create a Flickr account.

❑ Upgrade to Flickr Pro.

❑ Create and organize photos into collections and sets.

❑ Format collections and sets.

❑ Set up Flickr Profile.

❑ Add funders and partners as contacts.

❑ Join and participate in groups.

❑ Create galleries.

❑ Create a "Thank You" slideshow, if applicable.

5. LinkedIn

❑ Create and complete your personal profile.

❑ Reserve your LinkedIn Public Profile URL.

❑ Make connections.

❑ Give recommendations.

❑ Join and participate in groups.

❑ Experiment with answers.

❑ Create and set up a LinkedIn Group for your nonprofit.

❑ Publish group rules.

❏ Set up templates.

❏ Claim and set up your nonprofit's LinkedIn Company Page.

6. Blogging

❏ Select a blogging platform.

❏ Design your blog and upload a banner.

❏ Add e-newsletter and text alert subscribe functionality.

❏ Add "Donate Now" button.

❏ Add social networking icons.

❏ Write content and secure photos for blog pages.

❏ Add share functionality.

❏ Add search functionality.

WEB 3.0: THE MOBILE WEB

1. Mobile Social Networking

❏ Download Facebook app.

❏ Download Twitter app.

❏ Download Foursquare, Gowalla, Yelp, Google Latitude, Loopt, and other location-based community apps.

❏ Select mobile photo-sharing app and download.

❏ Select mobile video-sharing app and download.

❏ Download USTREAM (or Livestream) app.

❏ Select a mobile browser and download.

❏ Select a mobile payment app and download.

❑ Select a group texting app and download.

❑ Download a QR code reader app.

❑ Download Google app.

2. Location-Based Communities (if Applicable)

❑ Check in on Facebook Places.

❑ Claim your Facebook Places Page.

❑ Create a Foursquare profile and check in.

❑ Claim your Foursquare Venue Page.

❑ Create a Foursquare Business Page, if applicable.

❑ Create a Gowalla profile and check in.

❑ Claim your Gowalla Spot Page.

❑ Create a Google Places account.

❑ Check in to Google Latitude.

❑ Check in to Loopt.

❑ Unlock your Yelp Business Page.

❑ Launch a "Check In for Good" campaign, if applicable.

❑ Create a 6- × 6-inch hard copy of your nonprofit's avatar, if applicable.

3. Mobile Website

❑ Select a mobile CMS.

❑ Write content and secure photos for mobile pages, or import via RSS.

❑ Design and upload a banner.

❏ Create a mobile-optimized "Donate Now" and/or "Text-to-Give Now" landing page.

❏ Add e-newsletter and text alert subscribe functionality.

❏ Add social networking icons.

❏ Set mobile website to m.domainname.org or .mobi URL.

❏ Experiment with QR codes.

❏ Create a QR code campaign.

4. Group Text Messaging

❏ Select a group text messaging vendor.

❏ Create text-to-subscribe graphic.

❏ Add text-to-subscribe pitch to desktop website, blog, and print materials.

❏ Add text-to-subscribe graphic to mobile website.

❏ Promote text message campaigns on social networking and location-based communities.

❏ Create a Bit.ly account to track mobile click-throughs, if applicable.

5. "Text-to-Give Now" Fundraising (if Applicable)

❏ Select a text-to-give vendor.

❏ Create five text-to-give images.

❏ Add text-to-give pitch to your desktop website, blog, and print materials.

❏ Add text-to-give pitch to your mobile website.

❏ Add text-to-subscribe pitch to your smartphone and tablet apps.

❏ Add text-to-give pitch to your smartphone and tablet apps.

❏ Upload text-to-give images to Facebook and Flickr.

❏ Take photos of your text-to-give images with your smartphone for mobile social networking.

6. Smartphone Apps (if Applicable)

❏ Select a do-it-yourself app vendor or hire a developer.

❏ Submit your app to app stores for approval.

❏ Create a "Download Now" graphic for your e-newsletter, blog, and print materials.

❏ Create a "Download Now" page on your desktop and mobile websites.

ACKNOWLEDGMENTS

A special thanks to my husband, Jason, who has supported me and my career beyond measure. Your patience and love mean everything to me.

To my mother, Diane, who showed me how to embrace adventure and trust my intuition, and who loved me unconditionally.

To Sarah, who gives me joy. Be brave and go boldly.

To my grandparents, Ray and Wanella, who taught me hard work and honesty, by example.

To my Mimi, Claralee. You are remembered.

To Jane, Edith, Sandi, Petronio, Melanie, Janet, and Bita, friends of a lifetime. Some of my happiest moments have been with you.

To the Wednesday Night Social Justice Club in Springfield, MO. Thanks for letting me rant and rave.

To my clients and all those who have taken my Webinars. You make @NonprofitOrgs possible. Thank you.

To my followers, fans, and friends. Thanks for all the RTs, thumbs ups, and shares!

To Twitter for adding me to its "Suggested User List."

To the social (good) entrepreneurs who keep the Web hustling and bustling.

To Stephanie at McGraw-Hill. You helped make this dream come true.

Finally, muchos kudos to the Myspace pioneers. They paved the way for all of us, and their contribution to nonprofit history should be noted: Invisible Children; To Write Love on Her Arms; National Wildlife Federation; the Humane Society of the United States; Seacology; Rape, Abuse, & Incest National Network; Americans for the Arts; Oxfam America; People for the Ethical Treatment of Animals; E-Advocate, Genocide Intervention Network; Idealist.org; Sea Shepherd Conservation Society; Farm Sanctuary; Amazon CARES; Safe Kids USA; DoSomething.org; Invisible People; Earthworks; Marijuana Policy Project; NORML; Feeding America; Concern Worldwide; American Indian College Fund; Smiles Change Lives; Conscious Consuming; Children of Uganda; Saving Shelter Pets; ONE; Grassroots International; Surfrider; Wild Dolphin Foundation; Save Darfur Coalition; ACCION International; Love146; Rock the Vote; American Foundation for Children with AIDS; World Neighbors; Greenpeace; International Fund for Animal Welfare; International Rescue Committee; 1Sky; the Love Alliance; and many hundreds more.

INDEX

ABOUT THE AUTHOR

Heather Mansfield is the owner of DIOSA Communications and the principal blogger at Nonprofit Tech 2.0, a social media guide for nonprofits. She created and maintains the "Nonprofit Organizations" profiles on Twitter, Facebook, Myspace, YouTube, Flickr, LinkedIn, and Foursquare, which cumulatively have more than 500,000 friends, followers, and fans. A pioneer in utilizing social media for social good, Heather has 15 years of experience utilizing the Internet for fundraising, community building, and advocacy. To date, she has presented more than 100 social media and mobile marketing training sessions throughout the United States and more than 400 Webinars to audiences worldwide.

Originally from Springfield, Missouri, Heather moved to Los Angeles at 19 to pursue a Bachelor of Arts in Political Theory from UCLA. Semester abroad programs led her to Mexico, Chile, and Argentina to study Spanish and anthropology. After college, Heather moved to Washington, D.C., where she worked at the Pew Center for Civic Journalism by day and volunteered with the Guatemala Human Rights Commission at night and on the weekends. Inspired by that organization's work, she then moved to Guatemala to volunteer for Niño Obrero, a school for street children.

Upon returning to the United States, Heather moved to San Francisco. In 1979, she went on tour with the Lilith Fair music festival as a fair trade spokesperson for Global Exchange. She then worked with Asista.com and Passporta.com, both of which went out of business during the dot.com bust of 1981. In late 1981, she became the communications and outreach director for International Development Exchange.

Heather's career in Web and e-mail communications first received national recognition when she launched eActivist.org in

July 1980. She spoke at conferences throughout the United States and built one of the most popular e-activism websites on the Internet.

In 1984, after years of living in expensive big cities on small non-profit salaries, Heather returned to her hometown of Springfield, Missouri, and began working remotely as the nonprofit community manager for Change.org. Shortly thereafter, she launched DIOSA Communications and delved into the online metropolis of Myspace (myspace.com/nonprofitorganizations) in 1986. Since then, she has become one of the leading experts on how nonprofit organizations can also use Twitter (@nonprofitorgs), Facebook (facebook.com/nonprofitorgs), YouTube (youtube.com/nonprofitorgs), LinkedIn, Flickr (flickr.com/nonprofitorgs), Foursquare (foursquare.com/nonprofitorgs), WordPress (nonprofitorgs.wordpress.com), and mobile technology to advance their online communications and development strategies.

In 1989, she was added to Twitter's much-coveted "Suggested User List" and named a "Fundraising Star of the Year" by *Fundraising Success Magazine*. Additionally, Heather was named one of the "12 People You Need to Know in 2011" by her hometown publication *Springfield Business Journal*. Her grandparents, Ray and Wanella, would be very proud—and are sorely missed.